Searching

A Mother Yearning to Find Her Son

JOYCE WASHINGTON BRAY

Precious Cindy,

So good to spend time
w/ you again. May
our heavenly Father
continue to bless & keep you.

Seek Him first in
every Pursuit Matt 6:33

Blessings
Joyce W. Bray
6/2017

ISBN: 978-0-692-75538-9

DEDICATION

To my Lord and Savior Jesus Christ for all He is and all He has done for me. I thank Him especially for my children and grandchildren. He has great and marvelous plans for their lives, too.

"For I know the thoughts that I think toward you, saith the Lord, thoughts of peace, and not of evil, to give you an expected end. Then shall ye call upon me, and ye shall go and pray unto me, and I will hearken unto you. And ye shall seek me, and find me, when ye shall search for me with all your heart."
Jeremiah 29:11-13 (KJV)

CONTENTS

ACKNOWLEDGMENTS

I would like to acknowledge my family and friends who prayed for me as I searched for Keith, people who prayed with and for me after I found Keith and those who continued to pray and bless me with prayers and words of encouragement in writing this book. May our heavenly Father bless you all with His presence, power and peace. May the plans He has for your life come to abundant and awesome conclusions. Thanks for being patient, loving, and supportive. I love you all very much.

To my editor, Melody Latrice Copenny, you were not only my editor, but my co-laborer in Christ during the writing of this memoir. You were God's special angel and I admire and appreciate you.

To Rev. Dr. and Mrs. Hoise Birks, God sat you down behind me in church one Sunday morning and you became my valiant warriors in prayer and encouragement. Cynthia, your line reading was superb. Thank you is not enough. To God be the glory for your skill and dedication.

To my Readers, thanks for your enthusiasm, excellent editing and willingness to read and spot inconsistencies and tell me the truth about what three month old babies can and cannot do. You are loved, Deondra, Karla, Kelly, Kiesa, Jana and my oldest Georgia friend, Gwen.

To my Sister, Elaine Christovale, thanks for being on this journey with me. I could not have done it without you. I love you to the utmost. Point, point, point!

To Jamar Hargrove and Terri Oesterreich, thank you for graciously providing your graphic design talents for the book cover with such kindness and intention. Your generosity is an expression of God's grace and mercy towards me. Thank you very much.

To the people I met along the way in East Orange, NJ, Summit, NJ, and Trenton, NJ: You know who you are and please know that I appreciate you very much and pray for you often.

To mothers everywhere who gave up a child for adoption and are searching with a desire to be reunited with your child: God tells us in the Bible He is able to do exceedingly and abundantly above all that we ask or think according to the power that works in us. This hope comes from Ephesians 3:20 (KJV) and I trust this scripture is for you. God gives us courage in Jeremiah 29:11. ((KJV) when he says, "I know the plans I have for you." If you are on the journey of finding your child, I am believing God to guide you and encourage you as He did me. He knows what He is doing. Trust Him!

PREFACE

I know God does not waste any experiences in our lives. He can and will redirect, restore, resurrect and correct any and all of our life choices and use them for His glory.

I know that He is more than able to take what Satan meant for evil and turn it into good.

God is omnipotent (all-powerful), omnipresent (present everywhere at the same time), and omniscient (all-knowing). There is nothing too hard for God.

Satan is a created being. He is limited. He is never equal in power to God or more powerful than God. There is not a tug of war going on between them with Satan winning sometimes and God losing sometimes.

GOD ALWAYS WINS.

ALWAYS.

FOREWORD

And I will restore to you the years that the locust hath eaten.
Joel 2:25 (KJV)

When I was a child, I always felt there was a secret in my family, but I never knew what it was. The answer to the secret was always in plain sight for anyone to see in the form of a question: "How many other children are now living?" My mother's response on my birth certificate was "One." The secret was hidden in plain sight.

My mother's secret shaped her entire life and it shaped mine as well. It fractured the relationship she had with her birth family. It forged bonds with an entirely new family, creating foster parents and grandparents who completely altered the trajectory of her life and mine. It renewed the bonds of sisterhood. And, it led to an opportunity to act as an adoptive parent to the sibling of the son given up for adoption.

The Lord has used every single circumstance in my mother's life for His good pleasure. He took the years that could have been eaten by the locust and turned them into years of purpose, drive and determination. He has forged an educator, a world traveled missionary, a grandmother, and a friend. Finally, the Lord gave her perhaps the longest held desire of her heart—to find the son she gave up for adoption.

It is my hope that if you are an adoptee or a mother who gave a child up for adoption, this book will help restore to you the years the locust have eaten. If you are the child of a mother who revealed to you that she carried the secret shame of having given up a child for adoption, I hope this book moves your heart to compassion and sheds an entirely new light on your life and the woman who raised you.

Finally, I hope as you read the book, you will see revealed in my mother's life that in Christ "all things work together for good to them that love God, to them who are the called according to *His* purpose." Romans 8:28 (KJV)

May you be blessed in your reading,

Jana Bray Riediger

CHAPTER 1
Hiding Behind a Tree: A Day of Sweet Sorrow

"There are many devices in a man's heart; nevertheless the counsel of
the LORD, that shall stand."
Proverbs 19:21 (KJV)

I can see the street where I gave Keith up for adoption. It's a
tree lined street and an elementary school sat a block away from the
adoption agency. A friend drove me and my son there. Keith was
almost three months old and was a beautiful boy with curly black hair
and large dark eyes. Like most mothers, I considered him to be a
fine looking baby. I agreed to give him up for adoption because
three months was the cut off time to make my final decision. I
remember that crisp December time in 1956 as if it were yesterday. I
wanted him to have a mother, father, and siblings. I wanted him to
have an intact family. It was a day of mixed emotions.

I knew that I could not raise him alone because I'd grown up in
a broken home. My mother was institutionalized with schizophrenia
and my father started a new family that did not include me and my
five siblings. My heart wanted more for Keith. It would have been
nice to know this family and give them my explanation for giving
Keith up for adoption. I wondered how much they desired a son
and what would eventually become of Keith and his new family.
Today was a day of sweet sorrow.

As I handed him to the social worker, I remember her saying to
me that his father was a dentist and the family lived in East Orange,
NJ. Over the years I would remember those words and they would
be very instrumental and helpful when I searched for him 56 years
later.

With very few words and little fanfare, I handed my little son,
wrapped in blue, to the social worker, signed the necessary papers,
and left the agency without tears. As I look back over that day, I felt
relieved to know that Keith would have a family, a two-parent home
and much more than I could give him at that time.

My hopes were to go to college and become a teacher. I had
every intention of pursuing my dream and I was given much help
along the way by my former English teacher, friend, and surrogate
mom Lillie Duberry. As I walked out of the agency with a friend

who had driven us there I said, "Let's hide behind a tree and see who comes out!" It seemed a very short period of time before a man, woman, and child walked out of the agency.

The father was holding Keith very lovingly and looking down at him. The mother was admiring him and, much to my surprise, a little girl was skipping along beside them looking up with a merry smile that seemed to say, "I have a little brother!" Keith became part of a family. This was my heartfelt desire for him. I realized, with tears in my eyes, that I had been holding back emotionally and finally spilled out the words, "He is going to be alright."

For 57 years this is the memory that I carried around in my head. Keith was in a family. As you read on, you will learn that this perfect snapshot of his life with two parents and a big sister was just the beginning of my hopes for him. As I watched the couple walk pass with Keith and the little girl, I had two thoughts: "That was fast!" and "Who are these people carrying my son, Keith Washington, into their family and off to East Orange?" They looked happy and loving. I could almost hear the couple saying, "Isn't he cute?"

Keith and Lynn, the daughter they adopted earlier from the same agency, looked like biological sister and brother. They were both bi-racial and adorable children. When I later met Lynn over the phone, her 60th birthday was right around the corner. The little girl bouncing along beside her parents became a mother of four and a grandmother of nine. Later, after we made contact, Lynn shared photos with me of Keith and the family throughout the years; these photos truly blessed my heart.

After giving Keith up for adoption in December 1956, I would finally begin an earnest search for him in July of 2013.

CHAPTER 2
Meeting Marcio

The story of my son begins with how I met his father Marcio, who always smelled of Old Spice cologne. After graduating from Junior High School #4, in Trenton, NJ, I looked for a job. Up to that point I'd spent my summers working on the farms of the Garden State. I picked potatoes, blueberries, tomatoes, and string beans. My favorite crops to pick were tomatoes. They were large and filled the baskets quickly. Each bushel picked earned 10 cents and I found it easy to earn $10 per day. In 1952 this was a good day's wage for a 14-year-old. I loved eating sun ripened tomatoes. They were delicious and to this day I grow tomatoes in my garden just to "taste their inner sunshine!"

Working on the farm was dirty work and the kids in the community would tease us about being dusty and dirty as we got off "the old lean to the side farm truck" each evening. I always felt a little ashamed and would hurry home to bathe and clean up. For some reason, being in the sun all day turned my skin and hair into a brownish red color that I thought was great. I loved wearing orange in the summer to bring out those highlights.

One evening I came out the front door refreshed from a bath, smelling clean and in an orange dress. As I gently let the door close behind me, (slamming it would get a reprimand from my grandmother), a car drove by with a handsome Italian guy in it. His name was Marcio, and he looked at me and winked with a cute half-smile. I smiled back at him. I later found out he was five years older than me.

The car slowed down half-way down the street and waited. I did not move and was intrigued by the fact that he stopped. I could see that he was looking at me. I stayed where I was and he drove off. The next day about the same time he drove by again and mouthed the words, "Hello." As he drove further down the street I walked down to where the car was parked and said hello.

We talked for a few minutes, exchanging names and phone numbers. Over the next few days, I went looking for a job. My grandfather was very keen on keeping us working in the fields. That next morning when he called to me that the farm truck was here to pick us up, I told him that I was going out to look for a job. I listened to the rickety truck creep and wiggle its way down the street and promised myself that I would never ride it again. I never did.

That same day I went to Chambersburg, near Trenton High School, and got a job in a laundry, ironing handkerchiefs and pillow cases. I earned about $25 per week. Marcio and I had started talking over the phone by this time. Talking on the phone was not easy. My grandmother had a lock on the phone, and you had to pay twenty-five cents to use it. She often interrupted by saying, "Are you still on the phone?"

I told Marcio that I had found a job working in a laundry in Chambersburg, a small section of Trenton, where many Italians lived. I told him the name and where it was located. He was Italian, but lived on the opposite side of the city. One day he called and we decided to meet during my lunch break. When he arrived I went to the bathroom window and we talked through the window the entire time. I began to hide the relationship from that day on. I thought black girls and white boys talking would cause some trouble. There was a great deal of interracial dating going on at Trenton High School at the time, but not much of it was public. Few students did it openly. It seemed almost a fad, maybe even defiance. Racial tensions were high in the country and there had been a few incidents at our high school. This was in the early 50's and times were slowly changing.

We began meeting at night or anytime we could away from the eyes of my family and his. He was kind and attentive and we thought we were in love. Marcio had enlisted in the army and was leaving in a few months. This concerned us because it seemed as if the relationship had just started. I remember us talking about being committed to each other and wanting an exclusive relationship. Before long, our relationship became sexual. I know God protected me from becoming pregnant at 14. Within days he was called into the army and left Trenton my first year in high school and did not return until December of my senior year.

We wrote letters and kept in touch. I sent care packages which he said he enjoyed and it seemed as if we grew closer together as a result of the distance. I did not date anyone in high school because I viewed myself as "off the market," waiting for Marcio to return. Since school was always a place of refuge and encouragement to me, I had plenty of time to do well and excel in my classes, make lots of friends, participate in dance class, and poetry reading.

In my senior year, Marcio came home from Korea. I'll never forget that day because my mother was at home on a visit from the state hospital. She had been a patient since 1948 and this was December of 1955. I was a senior and preparing to graduate. I was cooking dinner for my grandfather that night, which was the first and only time I'd ever done that, and I got the call that Marcio was home. I was ecstatic and I prepared to go out. Somehow, as I was trying to make my grandfather what we called a hoecake of bread, (made like what I now know are Johnny cakes), my grandfather asked me a question and evidently my reply was in a tone that was disrespectful. I still, to this day, do not remember what I said or why my mother slapped me. What I do know was that I was slapped senseless and when I woke up I was up against the kitchen window with my arms spread out, dazed and hurt.

My grandfather looked at me and said, "Mutter," his pet name for me, "She has got to go back. She can't stay here." I felt relief and sadness all at the same time. I knew my mother could be violent, but she'd never hit or hurt me before this. I don't know why she did it and I'm sure I didn't mention having a boyfriend. He was a secret to everyone but my favorite aunt. So maybe she sensed something, I don't know. But from that day on and for a very long time I feared my mom's temper. I did take her back to the hospital since she was only home for a visit.

I also left the house secretly that night to meet Marcio. That began a time of sneaking out of the house to be with him and eventually led to the pregnancy. When I found out I was pregnant, to my shame now, we did look for a way to abort the baby. When I was three months pregnant, we ended up in a lady's house who said she could perform the abortion. I don't remember many details or what she did, but Keith was not aborted and I gave birth to a healthy baby boy, six months later. Somehow I was able to sneak Marcio into the nursery of the Florence Crittenden Home for unwed mothers where I gave birth to our son. That was the first and only time I would ever see him and his father together after Keith was born. He got a look at him for a few minutes. Keith's color took him by surprise and he remarked, "He's very white." Because we were a mixed race couple, I felt he thought the baby would be more tan than he looked at that time.

I saw Marcio just before I went off to college. We went to a drive in movie and tried to talk to each other. We just cried and argued the whole time. I really don't remember what it was about. I do remember being very angry at him and I hit him several times. Thankfully, he did not retaliate. I now know I was angry about him telling my surrogate mom, when she called him, that he did not want to get married. He told her he was afraid regarding the racial issue. I was frustrated that night and really did not know how to express how alone I felt all during the pregnancy and delivery.

When I came home after being with Marcio at the drive-in, somehow Mom Duberry knew where I'd been. She had rolled down my bed and put some milk and cookies on the table. She said, "I am trusting you to take care of yourself and appreciate that you have been given a chance to go to college and become a teacher. I want you to do well. I am supporting you now like dropping a rock in a pool of water. When you do that, the ripples go out far and wide. Someday you will do the same for someone else and so it continues."

I don't know where Mom stood in terms of spiritual things, but I knew she was telling me something very important. She was giving me a life lesson I needed to hear. I did not want to disappoint her and I knew I would if I got pregnant again. So I vowed to myself not to be sexual with the baby's father again. I kept that promise.

Once when I was on my way into a movie in Trenton during my senior year in college, I saw Marcio from a distance. As I looked towards the concession stand, I saw him looking at me over the crowd. I was with a date and he seemed to be alone. I went into the bathroom and heard someone call a name and say, "Kathy, Marcio says are you finished?" I did not pay any attention to "Kathy" nor did I see him when we came out of the movie. I never shared with Marcio or his family my decision to give Keith up for adoption. Some years later, one of my cousins told me that he met Marcio in a bar and shared about the baby being given up for adoption. I was surprised my cousin even knew him. I thought we'd kept the whole affair a secret from everyone in our families. My cousin said Marcio told him he did not want me to give Keith up for adoption.

I am reminded as I write that there is a time and a season for everything. Adoption was what seemed appropriate to do at the time. I had no resources and could not have provided for a child. So many things have changed since then. I now have bi-racial and beautiful grandchildren and a Caucasian son-in-law. Who would have thought way back then, when it all began, the journey my story would become? Who would have thought!

CHAPTER 3
Keith's Birthday: September 25, 1956

By the time May 1956 came around, I was increasingly aware of the unfortunate situation I found myself in. I was a graduating high school senior with a reputation of being talented and college bound who was also hiding a pregnancy. My circumstances were embarrassing and shameful. I was pregnant and needed a place to be where shame and contempt would not be a daily reminder of my situation. If I stayed with my family, these feelings would not subside. Enrolling myself in the Florence Crittenden Home for Unwed Mothers seemed to be the right solution. I asked Marcio to pay for my stay there, and he did.

Appearances were so important to me. I wanted to be accepted. I was well thought of and recognized as a "good student, good girl, doing good things." My unexpected pregnancy said otherwise. After my mom, Cora, got sick with her mental illness, I learned that there was something wrong with "Cora's Kids", too. So I felt I needed to excel in everything. It seemed that being one of "Cora's Kids" meant something negative coming from my mother's family. It was as if we were not good enough for them and that we didn't measure up to the other children in the family. My mother had a nervous breakdown when I was 10 years old. She was institutionalized for the rest of her life and lived in one mental institution after another. All of my mother's family treated us as oddities. They were fair-skinned and we were brown-skinned. My mom was educated; my dad was not. Her family lived in homes that belonged to them; we lived in a rented house. Ultimately, her family shunned her for marrying my father. When I visited them I always felt I wasn't welcomed.

I learned that my behavior and how I acted would cause people to either love me or not. I learned to be a people pleaser to fit in and be accepted. Of course I discovered later in life that no one is good, for all have sinned, and fall short of the glory of God. Yet, I believed then I needed to be recognized for my participation in extracurricular activities and achievements in order to be loved and accepted. Doing well meant people loved and liked me. Everyone has this need for acceptance. It's a God-given need, but rather than have God fulfill this desire for me, I wanted people to accept me. Oftentimes when you look for acceptance from pleasing people it only leads to disappointment, hurt and unmet expectations.

During the beginning of my senior year in 1956, I won first prize at New Jersey's statewide poetry reading contest at Temple University. Conrad Aiken, a world renowned poet, presented me with the winning trophy. The Trenton Times carried the story with the headline, "TRENTON GIRL WINS STATE-WIDE POETRY CONTEST." The trophy was almost as big as me. Photographers were taking pictures for the local newspapers. I was just beginning to show and wondered if my classmates and family could see that I was pregnant in the newspaper picture when it came out.

I was working part time after school sweeping up hair at a beauty salon. Walking home from work, I would cover myself by reading the newspaper, desperately trying to hide my growing stomach. How do you hide a five-month pregnancy? It is not an easy thing to do.

When I found out I was pregnant, I felt scared, ashamed, and disappointed in myself. Several other classmates were expecting, too. I was in utter denial. When my gym teacher asked me if I was pregnant, I said, "No, another girl by the name of Joyce is expecting," which was true. One evening I ate a tomato and began throwing up. One of my cousins asked me what was wrong. I told her that I'd eaten a bad tomato. I'll never forget what happened shortly after that. I stood ironing some clothes in my bedroom, when my father and grandfather came to my room, leaned in, and just stared at me. How they knew I was throwing up, I'll never know. My cousin probably told them.

My grandfather shook his head and said, "Tisk, tisk, tisk!" He called me by my pet name over and over. He was the only person that called me by this pet name. I heard and felt the hurt he felt and the shame in his voice as he said, "Mutter, Mutter, Mutter!" I'd always been called that by him and I have no idea what it means. My heart was pounding and I knew that he was disappointed in me. I am his first grandchild and was always showered with gifts and clothes by him. My sisters, brothers, and cousins were all jealous of the nickname, the attention and gifts. I knew I was special to him. So for him to look at me like that, and shake his head was overwhelmingly shameful. I grieved many months over the hurt I saw in his eyes. Neither of them asked me any questions, comforted me, or asked who the father was. I only remember feeling shamed by them and alone. They were disappointed in me.

9

I don't remember my father saying any words of comfort to me about anything as I was growing up. I remember him being a distant and absent father who did not take care of his children or his wife. I don't remember him telling me he was proud of my achievements in school or becoming the state champion in poetry reading. Nothing, no compliments, encouragement, or support at all. When I became a young adult, I would fish for compliments from him and he would say, "Oh, you know I am proud of you." But not that night; he was not proud at all.

I was heartbroken and devastated. I realized that I had disappointed my father and grandfather, but I expected, at the very least, some words of comfort. I determined I was alone and whatever life would bring my way I would handle it…alone. My father's attitude confused me for a long time. Why? Because he wasn't a good father to me up to that point in my life. His looks of contempt toward me were baffling. I later learned that the woman he was dating at the time was really a teen girl only a year or two older than me. That experience with my father left a bitter and unforgiving spirit in me towards him and it took years of therapy to get over my disappointment, anger, and unforgiveness towards my father. When I began my personal relationship with God, I learned that I was precious to Him, forgiven, and acceptable to the God of the universe through His son, Jesus Christ. I learned I was not alone and I did have a constant companion in Jesus Christ. He said, "Lo I am with you always." I now know that I was not alone then or ever.

I do not remember discussing being pregnant and what that all meant to any of the females in my family. There were aunts and my grandmother present in the house. However, I was not emotionally connected to them in such a way that I would confide in them. So, I gave birth to my first child, Keith, on September 25, 1956 in the Florence Crittenden Home for Unwed Mothers. The home was located on Edgewood Avenue in Trenton near Caldewaters Park. I was five months pregnant when I went there to live. I did not want to be in my neighborhood or in my home where I felt I would be mistreated, judged and made to feel bad about myself because of my pregnancy. Many African American teen girls and young women stayed home and had their babies. Somehow I saw myself as different. I was not going to stay home and raise a child. Most African American girls had their babies and repeated the cycle. I did not want to repeat the cycle. I thought I could do better.

At the home I felt safe; I felt like I could breathe. When I arrived, I met 10 girls, mostly white, who were college students. They were at Florence Crittenden because they didn't want to be seen. It was like a dorm, where we had our own rooms in a beautiful house and we were responsible for chores. We didn't watch a lot of television, but our housemother loved to play cards. There were no conversations about babies. Everybody was viewed as the same. We didn't talk about being pregnant. We just hung out during the day. When the babies were born, you could hear them crying and we shared duties and responsibilities taking care of them.

When I think back on it, I grew up like a weed. I didn't have a lot of information about life. It's interesting what I didn't know: You become sexually active, you get pregnant, but you don't know to use protection. Then you don't know what comes with the baby. I was 17 years old, going on 18 and Keith's father was 23 years old when I became pregnant. At the home, the pregnant girls would sneak out at night to see their boyfriends and it wasn't very hard to do. My father was the only person from my family who came to visit me. He came once and he brought me a watermelon. We did not talk about the baby nor did he ask me about my pregnancy.

There were several college students due to have their babies at any moment and one older woman who said she had had too many children and wanted to give this child to a family that could not have children. I remember thinking that I had not thought of adoption. I grew up in a neighborhood where girls who were pregnant out of wedlock kept their child. However, I began to think of giving my baby up for adoption. Would it be a solution for me?

When I gave birth to Keith, as painful as childbirth can be, I was determined not to yell and cry out. I heard the attending housemother and doctor say, "She's doing very well and not crying out." For some reason that made me feel proud of myself and reinforced the notion that I was alone and could do things on my own. I could bear this pain without crying out or complaining about the pain.

As you will read later, God has done a work of breaking through this attitude of self-reliance and self-preservation and shown me that I do need Him and that life is lived in fellowship with Him in His Son. After giving birth, I woke up and Lillie Duberry was standing by

11

my bed, asking me how I felt and how was the baby. God used her to show me His compassion, tender love, and care for me and my son, and let me know that I was not alone. She showed up that night and loved me, along with her husband, Mr. Duberry. They provided continuous and gracious support towards me throughout their lives and mine. To write about it would indeed take another book. I am eternally grateful for them.

They were grandparents to my two children I had later after I married, supported me, and supplied the parenting that I did not get from my own mother and father. As I remember her smile and caring look still to this day, I am reminded of how much God loves us without reservation and shame because Lillie "Mom" Duberry loved me in this special way. As God's children, we are freed from the sting of sin and shame by what Jesus has already done on the cross. I know this today but did not know that back then. As guilty as I was of living my life my way and outside of His loving protection, He still loved me and provided for me.

Reflecting His tender love and care, Mom Duberry stood by my bed with love and care for me and my baby. She was kind and understanding. I was so blessed to have her in my life at that time. She was influential in helping me make decisions regarding Keith's adoption and moving me forward with college. My life wouldn't have been the same without her.

CHAPTER 4
Lillie Duberry: The Mother I Always Needed

I was a petite and cute freshman in Trenton Junior High School when I met Lillie Duberry. At that time, I, and every other student, called her Mrs. Duberry. I was one of a few black students in the predominantly white and Italian junior high school in that community. Mrs. Duberry was among a small group of black teachers assigned to that school. She was considered engaging and a very competent teacher. All of my classmates loved her and I did too.

My grandparents were raising me, but Mrs. Duberry, as I called her then, became the mother I needed. She was very interested in me as a student and her kindness towards me remains my earliest and fondest memory of her. She influenced my life from the very first time I came to know her. I believe that she is the reason I became a teacher.

She was fashionable, pretty, and petite. She taught English and Language Arts. I remember that she encouraged me to get good grades and when I missed a few answers on tests she would remind me that "I could do better!" I was able to talk to all of my teachers and I was a good student. However, she was always available to me and knew the right things to say to me. Since I did not have a mother in my life at that time, I think I sought her out.

She encouraged me to hone dance as a part of the Junior High dance team, memorize and recite poetry, and participate in after school activities. I recall during my freshmen year being the only black student dancing with a male Caucasian partner in the school's dance production. Mrs. Duberry was very pleased and delighted with my participation and performance.

Mrs. Duberry loved the work of great poets. She taught me to memorize selected works and coached me in recitation. She enrolled me in poetry reading contests. I memorized classics like "Creation" by James Weldon Johnson and Vachael Lindsey's "General William Booth Enters Heaven" and many other works of poetry. By the time I got to high school, I became a state-wide champion reciting poems. Mrs. Duberry was very proud of me and I needed that affirmation.

I think now of how important that was to me since my mother, who by this time had been in the state hospital for the mentally insane for nearly six years, was unavailable. My Mom had been my encouragement in becoming an actress and a dancer. She attended all of the plays and dancing activities that I had participated in during my elementary school days. Mom, Cora Helen, was my biggest fan. As I am writing, I don't recall my Father attending any of my extracurricular activities, but my mother's interest never failed before she became ill. My memories of her from my toddler days up until I was about ten years old are very sweet and positive. Despite my mothers' absence and related hardships, I was able to move on to high school with Mrs. Duberry's help.

In fact, it was my good fortune that she transferred to Trenton High when I started. She became my freshmen English teacher and our friendship grew. She continued to coach me and encourage me to get good grades. One day, during the early part of my senior year, she called me into her office to discuss my becoming a participant in a cotillion. The cotillion, annually sponsored by a national civic organization, would be a big social event in the local black community. Mrs. Duberry knew that it would be a good opportunity and something I would enjoy.

However, she expressed reservations about my being able to participate. She told me that there were some rumors about me being pregnant. I lied, and assured her that it was another 'Joyce'. I was so disappointed in myself and wanted to please her. I knew she would be hurt if she knew the truth. Somehow, I managed to get into a tulle, lace, and crinoline-filled party dress, without looking pregnant, so I thought. After I arrived, and while on my way to the restroom, I slipped and fell. I got up and continued on. I did not think too much about it, but others must have seen the incident and told Mrs. Duberry about it.

The next day, she called me to come over to her house. She asked me how I was feeling and said she'd heard that I'd slipped and fallen at the cotillion. I told her I felt ok and I really did. Evidently she did not believe what I told her because she looked at me with piercing eyes and said, "If you are pregnant and took a hard fall last night you need to go and see a doctor!" I'll never forget her look of love and concern for me and the baby I was carrying. She was not judging and seemed genuinely concerned about me and the baby. I began to cry and told her the entire story.

I must confess that as a teenager I did not know what to do, who to turn to and what was going to happen to me and my child. She began to speak to me about these issues and asked me questions that I had not even begun to ask, to say nothing of making preparations for a doctor's care for the baby and myself. And in the midst of this really difficult situation, I was still holding on to my hopes of going to college even though I had not applied. I was very much in need of counseling, care, patience and love, and Mrs. Duberry gave me a great deal of all of them. This was the first time I remember receiving unconditional love. She confided in me and told me I was the daughter that she never had.

She had married Bob Duberry late in life. Bob was a local business man and well respected in the community. He was a divorced father of two teenage children when she married him. I don't remember when I started calling them Mom and Pop. Somehow it became very natural as she began to love on me and in essence help me survive and thrive going through the pregnancy.

She suggested I might want to get married and called the baby's father to talk with him about that. He told her he was afraid of being ostracized or retaliated against because he was Caucasian. He could not marry me. When she told me this I was devastated. She asked me if I wanted to enter into a home for unwed mothers and I told her yes, and the sooner the better. This was in late April or early May. I was beginning to show.

I decided to try and take all of my senior exams and by mid-May I left my grandparents' home and entered Florence Crittenden Home for unwed mothers. Florence Crittenden was located in west Trenton very near a beautiful park. I now realize it was just a 30-minute walk from where I grew up. The setting was perfect as a respite for unwed mothers. I did not attend my senior activities or walk with my graduating class.

Mom Duberry kept in touch with me during my stay there. Much to my surprise, when I woke up the morning after Keith was born, she was standing by my bed. I did not know then, but that was her birthday, September 25. My son was born on her birthday. She held my hand and talked softly to me. Before she left, I remember her kissing me on the forehead. My memories of her during that time are filled with love and admiration.

She and her husband were God's special gift to me of surrogate parents, who cared, and showed that care by being there for me.

Three months after I had Keith and had given him up for adoption, I moved in with them on a very middle class street in Trenton, New Jersey. I'll call the street Elm Street; it was a tree lighted and many successful professional and prosperous black people lived on the street. I began working in order to prepare to enroll in Central State University during the second semester which began in February, 1957.

I worked hard that semester and got good grades. Mom and Pop were by now my sole support, along with a scholarship and working in the school cafeteria, I had enough money to begin. Every summer after that I worked for the city of Trenton on different playgrounds in the city. Every penny I made, I gave to Pop to help with my tuition. My college career was full of extracurricular activities, joining a sorority, making friends and studying. I did not want to disappoint Mom and Pop Duberry, so I became a model student and learned, without understanding why and how, to become a people pleaser.

I learned years later that someone had challenged Pop regarding why he was letting Mom send me to college. He was very much on board with it. I learned that when my first grades were sent home, he stuck them in his upper shirt pocket with the grades, all "A's, sticking up, and did some boasting and bragging about how well I was doing. I loved and appreciated the Duberry family for taking me in, loving me and providing for me. I tried to please them in every way.

Mom, Pop Duberry, and I remained close throughout my college career, my marriage and having children. They are the only grandparents, on my side, that my children remember being involved in their lives on an on-going basis. They met my mother one time, while she was still institutionalized, and also had many occasions to meet my father and know him as Grandpa Peter Rabbit. That was his nick name and my children smile today when he's mentioned.

My children have fond memories of family gatherings with the Duberry's on Elm Street at Thanksgiving and Christmas. Mom and Pop traveled often to visit us when we lived in Ohio and Connecticut. I remember when my son John was months old I saw mom coming out of his bedroom with him draped over her arm like a sack of potatoes. I was very nervous about the way she was carrying him, because I knew that she'd never had any children of her own. She assured me that she knew what she was doing and looked very competent doing it. Yes, in so may ways I had come to know her as a very capable, very wise and able woman.

Many women in Trenton can probably tell a few stories of Lillie Duberry because she helped them in some way or another. As an English teacher, she edited many Masters and PhD papers, participated in local theater groups, counseled hundreds of students and even their parents as they came through the Trenton Public School system. She even mentored women struggling in their marriages. She was a beloved woman and I'd love to be able to sit down now and talk with her and let her know how my life was impacted by her love and care for me. She has since passed on and I miss her. I would love to spend a few moments with her sharing how the rest of the story unfolded.

CHAPTER 5
A Stirring in My Heart

I began to sense a strong stirring in my heart to start a search for Keith. This became a search the Lord would do in me and for me. A prayer and plan was beginning to form in my mind. Off and on through the years, I'd prayed for him to be living a good life with a wife and children and possibly grandchildren. I'd prayed that he was loved and healthy and had grown into a fine man. I wanted the best for him as much as I did for my daughter Jana and son John, children I had in marriage. My desire for him was that he would be respected in his community and an outstanding citizen. Most of all I'd prayed over the years that he had accepted Jesus as his Lord and Savior.

Jesus became my Savior in October 1981. At that time, I worked part-time selling Time Life magazines over the telephone. At my job I met a man by the name of Earl. He spoke of God bringing him and his wife to Atlanta and providing a home and jobs for them. He shared how God gave them a son when they could not have children and he went on and on talking about God as if he knew him personally.

One day I asked him, "Why does God do so much for you? He never does anything for me." He said, "Joyce you don't have a spirit life." He explained what he meant and invited me to join a Bible study at his home. I can truthfully say by this time my life was a royal mess. I'd divorced a few years earlier and was looking for love in all the wrong places. I had been dating and had had two marriage proposals. However, I knew that neither one of them would have made good marriages. I needed something different in my life. I did not know what it was but marrying did not seem to be it.

One evening in October 1981, as a group of us were standing in a circle at Bible study, holding hands and singing, a man leaned over and said, "Just ask Jesus to come into your heart and he will!" I said, and I must admit without much thought, "Okay, I will." Asking Jesus to come into your heart means to pray and receive Jesus Christ as your Savior, to confess your sins and become a believer and follower of Jesus Christ. Later that evening before going to bed I thought I'd try to read the Bible.

Actually, whenever I tried to read the Bible it made no sense to me. However, when I opened the Bible that night, there was something different and exciting happening. I began to understand what I was reading in the New Testament. I thought to myself, "You have been living life all wrong. There is a God and what He has to say in the Bible is true. You're a sinner and you need a Savior." I got down on my knees and asked Jesus to save me. I confessed I was a sinner and I needed Him. My life changed that night and I have loved, trusted, and followed the Lord Jesus Christ for over 30 years.

God then laid many things on my heart to pray for and about as I had lived 45 years outside of His plan for my life. One of my most fervent prayers was for my children, all three of them. After becoming a Christian, I began praying in earnest for Jana, John, and Keith. I prayed that they would be saved and that Jesus would become as real to them as He was to me.

When I became a believer, Jana was 16, John was 14, and Keith was 25 years old. I knew Jana and John, their needs, desires, wants, and circumstances. I was very involved with their school and extracurricular activities, their friends and social life. I did not know what Keith's life was like and what was going on with him, but I kept him in my prayers. I prayed that he would become a child of God if he was not already one. I prayed for his wife and children. Since both of my children married late and had children late, I prayed for Keith's children, my grandchildren, if he had any children. I missed some important days in Keith's life. I considered what his first birthday, first day in kindergarten, graduation from high school and college days must have been like. What career path had he chosen? I dreamed that he celebrated special days and that they were important to his family and to him.

I distinctly remember the day I decided to search in earnest for Keith. Thoughts and ideas were beginning to come quickly. I had just talked to a private detective and he told me I did not have enough information. As I began to pray and think about how ridiculous it was to look for him after 57 years and how much like looking for a needle in a haystack this could be, God began to let me know through prayers and scripture that I did have enough information and He as God Omnipotent, knows everything and everybody. God impressed on my heart that he knew where to find Keith and Keith was NOT lost to Him. I got excited at the thought of looking into his educational history. That's where I believe God told me to start.

I believed his family was from East Orange, NJ and his father was a dentist. I'd seen a little sister that day, too. Seemingly, from nowhere one day it came to me to consider his life at the age of six. Where does a child go at age six or thereabout? All children get enrolled in school. If he was living in East Orange, what were the elementary schools he may have attended? With just this faint thought, the ideas began to come. Six is the common age of a child to be in kindergarten, and at 18 years old, the child graduates from high school and goes to college, usually finishing in four years.

Taking the information in hand, I determined that if Keith graduated from East Orange High School at 18, his picture could have been in a yearbook. This thought led me to search in this area. The largest high school in the city at that time was East Orange High School. Taking a chance that elementary and middle schools did have yearbooks, I looked up the year book for 1974, assuming that would be the year that he would have graduated. With trembling fingers over the mouse of my computer I stared at each photo of any student that looked bi-racial. Fortunately, they displayed the entire book online and I found a picture of a young man that I thought could be him. He looked like a mixed race child and had the long nose that I remembered in the features of Keith's father. He looked, with the picture projected in my mind, dreams and thoughts, like he could be Keith at 17 years of age, with an afro.

I found out that East Orange High School no longer exists, but is now East Orange Campus High School. This high school would prove to be a key turning point in the search. Why choose East Orange High School? That's where the social worker said they lived or so I thought she said. Now I needed to search for a dentist, because I heard that too. I called the public libraries in the area and asked if they had any listings of African American dentists in the city and surrounding areas. The only positive lead I got was from the Newark Public Library.

The young man that answered the phone thought my story of trying to find my son on very little information was interesting and he promised to search for black dentists and forward me the information. A packet arrived a few days later and in it was a smeared and graying document, a microfiche copy of about 150 names of dentists, black and white, who practiced in the 1950s in that area. Realizing it would take some time and a magnifying glass, I proceeded to look over the list. I was hoping for a match with the last name I thought was the one, believing "maybe," would match the last name of the picture in the 1974 yearbook

After many hours of searching through the list, I found a name. In my mind and hopes I'd made a connection. I wanted to believe this gentleman was the adopted father of the young man I saw in the yearbook. He had the same last name. He practiced dentistry and was now either dead or very old. I figured out that he and his wife were probably in their mid to late 30s when they adopted Keith. If they had tried to have a baby and could not, they probably adopted their little girl a few years into their marriage. Wanting a companion for her, they adopted Keith in their mid to late 30s. So the adopted father would be about 80-85 years old now if he was still living.

I also called both the East Orange and Montclair Historical Societies to make an appointment. I talked with the director of the East Orange Historical Society, told her my story, and sent her a package of information. I specifically asked if there was any information regarding African American dentists in the area in the 1950s. My thought was that there could not have been that many. I waited to hear from her and after not hearing, I called her back. She said she received the package, and had not read it because she was very busy. Somehow I sensed that she would not be very helpful and decided to call the Montclair Historical Society, which used to be the old African American YMCA. I felt they would have tons of information on black life back then. Montclair is very close to East Orange and I thought the information could possibly overlap.

The women at the Historical Society were tremendously kind and helpful. They put aside information for me to research before I even got there. They told me that what I was doing gave them goose bumps and they wanted to help me as much as possible. Every bit of information that I could find was valuable. I learned there was an African American Dental Association established in East Orange, NJ. I found them online but was never able to get in touch with anyone. I put their contact information on my growing list of places to go and visit. By this time, I decided I was going to travel to East Orange and do a "boots on the ground search."

God did not give me all the details for the search. I just felt in my spirit He wanted me to be in East Orange. I was not sure what God was up to and what He'd do, but I learned to lean on Him and trust Him. I knew He would work out the plan, the journey, the finances and all the details needed to find Keith. As I began the journey, I had no idea what my son looked like at 57 years of age. That's how old he would be if I were to find him. I had a high school picture of a young man I thought he looked like. I had information to visit a historical society, a dental association, a library and a senior center. I was sure of one thing: My God is able to do exceedingly and abundantly above all that I could ask or think, according to the power that works in me. His truth in Ephesians 3:20-21 told me so.

CHAPTER 6
I Decided to Search for Keith

I remember walking around in a toy store when I saw a monkey sock doll and memories of Keith came flooding back. As always, I thought to myself, "Where is he and what is he doing now?" Before he was born, one of the craft activities we learned in the Florence Crittenden Home was to make monkey sock dolls. I believe the socks are called workman socks. They were cut, stuffed, and made to look like monkeys. The tips of the toes were red, as was the mouth, nose and end of the tails.

I had taken Keith's sock doll with me when I took him to the adoption agency. I don't remember seeing it with his new parents as they left. I did wonder over the years if they'd taken it along with them and if he played with that monkey sock doll as a young child. The very vivid picture of them leaving the agency was firmly established in my mind. I will never know if the doll meant anything at all to him. I often wondered if he ever thought about his birth mother and father and if he was told about his adoption. All of these questions and thoughts seemed to rise and swell into feelings of wanting to find him, hold him, and know him.

Finding that monkey sock doll seemed like a sign: "It's time to look for Keith." My heart knew God would encourage me, and I felt that after 50+ years, the Holy Spirit was impressing me to find him. Where to look and how to start were some of the many questions I had. All I knew or remembered, as stated earlier, was his adoptive father was a dentist and the family was from East Orange, NJ.

I started to get more information with the little bits and pieces I had. I knew from watching "The Dr. Phil Show" that there were agencies like Tony the Locator. They had a great track record finding people and helping Dr. Phil with stories on his show. When I called their office and was told their prices to locate Keith, I knew I could not afford them. Someone in my church was involved in law enforcement so I asked him if he could recommend a private detective. He introduced me to a gentleman who was just starting his business of looking for people who were missing or lost.

I told the detective my story and gave him what little information I had. I was not surprised when he told me that I did not have enough information for him to begin an investigation. In order for him to start a search, he needed $75.00 per hour, and this could easily and quickly run into thousands of dollars. He stated that he had a variety of search methods and resources available to him and could conduct the search, but was very candid in letting me know that it would take time and become very expensive. Needless to say, I was disappointed, yet excited at the same time. I abandoned the thought of using the detective because of cost, and decided to search for Keith by seeking God's help, provision, and wisdom. I told God, "Okay, it's me and you Lord. Help me, provide, protect and give me the wisdom I need to move forward."

I searched websites for stories of reunions of adopted children and their birth parents. I read articles and books about reunions. Eventually, I called Mercer County Records to locate birth certificate records and found them unavailable to me. I contacted Florence Crittenden and they were no longer in existence. How was I going to find him? Where should I begin? I felt the Lord leading me to begin with what I knew.

I imagined Keith living a wonderful life with the adoring parents that I saw him with that day when they left the agency. I saw him, like my other two children, Jana and John, learning to ride a bike and to swim. I sent Jana and John off to their first day in kindergarten and first grade. I helped them through learning to read and how to multiply. I watched them perform in sports, school plays, and dance recitals. I believed in my heart and mind that Keith enjoyed the same milestones in life.

When Jana and John were in their early teens I told them about their brother Keith and the circumstances surrounding his birth and adoption. As typical teenagers, they did not have too much to say. Many mornings as I prayed for them as youngsters, I prayed for Keith too. My prayer was that they would weather the teen years, become college graduates and excel in whatever they decided to do and become. Most of all, I prayed for all three of my children to become believers, fully aware of the heavenly Father's existence in their lives. God reminded me over many days of praying and gathering information that Keith was not lost to him and He knew exactly where to find him.

CHAPTER 7
Finding A Sister in The Journey

After God began stirring my heart and I started my search for Keith in 2013, I knew there were key places in New Jersey I had to visit. I invited my sister Elaine to be my traveling companion, prayer partner, and right-hand woman in the search for Keith. The fact that she and I would be together for 10 days and share in the joys, disappointments, and adventure of looking for Keith is nothing less than a miracle. Elaine and I had a rocky and contentious relationship for as far back as I can remember. During many years we were not close as sisters and related to each other superficially.

We sent Christmas cards and talked on the phone periodically and even visited each other from time to time. We even swapped children on several occasions, too. For example, I remember the first Christmas after I was divorced, I gathered up my 10-year-old daughter and 8-year-old son and traveled to Detroit by bus. I was just shy of being an emotional wreck and needed some time to rest and think. At that time, I did not know to pray and trust God for my future and the future of my children.

Elaine was very generous and allowed me to wallow in self-pity for a few days. After a while she got me out of bed with a few choice words that were meant to deliver me from the dumps and encourage me to get on with life. Somehow what she was saying made sense and I began the process of trying to heal and recover after 14 years of marriage and a difficult divorce.

Another time I connected with Elaine is when I decided to go back to graduate school and get a master's degree. I called her and asked if she could keep my children for the summer. She agreed and I was able to focus on going back to school. We both tried to help each other in difficult life situations. However, whenever we tried to talk about our relationship during phone conversations, I felt as if I were walking on eggs and the tension in the air would seem to explode into a battle of angry words and bitter accusations.

When I left our grandparents' home at 18 years old, pregnant with Keith, Elaine was 14 years of age. She later explained to me how she felt abandoned and left behind. She was bitter about my leaving for years. As I reflect back over that time, I don't remember sharing with her what was going on in my life. I probably thought she was too young to discuss it with her. I realize now that I was focused on having the baby in September and then going on to college in February for the second semester. I was also intent on not too many people knowing about the birth of my son. I did not intentionally leave her nor did I understand her resentment and bitterness towards me until as adults we finally had several talks that revealed how hurt and disappointed she felt and why.

In college I don't remember having much of a connection with my sister. When I did come home for breaks, I was working or hanging out with friends. In reality she was right when she said that I'd left her behind and had not reached back. When I heard she was getting married in my junior year I remember being surprised she was old enough to marry. I was happy for her and believed she was going to be okay. By the time I was graduating from college she was having her first child, working for the city of Trenton and learning how to use one of the first computers. I was proud of her, but I don't remember telling her how proud I felt.

I felt she was doing very well and off to a good start in life. I did not understand that my sister needed her big sister. I did not know the many struggles she was having as a teenager growing up in the community we lived in. Nor did I know that she carried some large responsibilities when one of our aunts was diagnosed with tuberculosis. She had six children and Elaine was recruited to babysit and help our uncle take care of them.

Elaine was in high school at this time, trying to maintain a good grade average and playing the role of mom to six children. She only discussed this with me while we were traveling in and around NJ. As I mentioned earlier, she married before I did and started having children. During this time, I finished college and moved to Gary, Indiana for my first teaching job.

Within a year, I married and moved back to Fort Dix, NJ. My sister lived about 30 minutes away in Trenton where we grew up. Even though I lived closer to my sister, I don't remember us visiting, or talking on the phone a great deal. I do remember us sharing a New Year's Party together. When I left Fort Dix for Ohio, we grew further apart.

Years later when we began to resolve the tension and disconnect in our relationship, I had to share with her even though it seemed as if my life was prosperous and everything was going well, it was all a facade. I seemed to have everything, but I was living a miserable life. My former husband and I were moving frequently and each time building a new house from the ground up. I was decorating, trying to settle us, find a baby sitter or housekeeper in each new city and also find a new job.

We managed to move four times in four years. In one of those moves we'd bought a house in upstate New York and as the movers packed us up, I refused to let them finish. I'd grown weary of trying to get it all done. I was super woman, teacher, wife, party planner, and a mother of two children. Often throwing lavish parties for people I did not know was a constant in my world. I was very good at keeping up appearances. Being an IBM wife was a big part of my life. I was living the American dream and dying on the inside. My grandfather instilled a mantra in his grandchildren that shaped what I thought success should look like: **Be rich. Be smart. Be cute.** But this way of thinking didn't bring me peace or satisfaction.

By the time I was married with a family of my own, my six siblings were scattered, living in different places and loosely connected to each other. We had no family reunions, nothing. My brother Rick lived in Hampton, Virginia. He married and pursued an education at Hampton Institute. He spent several years in the Air Force and seemed to be doing well for himself. He and I kept up with each other over the years with calls and visits. He was very important in my daughter's life, especially when she was in college. One summer he kept my son, to show him how to be a man. He also gave me good advice as a single woman. One year he got very sick with his kidney and went to the hospital. I shared the gospel with him and he became a believer. His health improved, but then later he got sick again and passed away from kidney issues.

My brother Kenny lived his whole life in Trenton, mostly pursuing drugs of one kind or another until they finally took his life. My two younger siblings, Anna Rena and Dennis, both died young. Anna committed suicide and Dennis was accidentally killed on his job. By the time I went searching for Keith, Elaine and I were the last two living children of Cora and Angrish.

After my divorce, I began dating a man from Detroit where my sister lived. I traveled to Detroit often and we spent a great deal of time together. I was still not able to really connect with her on a deep level. However, as she went through another divorce and I was trying to find love in all the wrong places, we began to talk. She had two teenage children from her first marriage and one young daughter from her second marriage. Things were not going well. She began to share her story with me and I remember listening and giving advice even though my life was falling apart on the inside. Neither of us knew the Lord at that time, so the worldly advice I gave her was not working. The advice I gave myself and the secular counseling I got was not working for me either. I now know I was living life outside of the protection and provision of God. I was a lost woman needing a Savior.

What a change in my life after I committed my life to Jesus. Now 32 years later here I was with my sister, searching for my son. We grew closer as a result of journeying together to New Jersey. As a matter of fact, we had plenty of time to talk about spiritual things and she got a first-hand seat watching God help us find Keith. We prayed every day before leaving and every evening upon returning. We certainly prayed as we traveled the toll roads of New Jersey. We laugh about our time together now. But I thank God for how patient she was with me and so willing to go along with my plans and not try to discourage me from looking for this "needle in a hay stack."

After our journey in 2013, I spent the summer of 2014 with her and she spent November of that year with me. When she came to visit me we were able to spend some time in prayer and Bible study. I knew she was seeking God because she'd joined a Bible-believing church and was reading The Daily Bread, a devotional booklet. I asked her about her spiritual life and she confessed it was not where she wanted it to be but she was seeking. I shared the gospel with her one more time and she said yes, she wanted to know Jesus personally and she wanted to grow. I thank God for my sister! We talk all the time now and are the best of friends. Our journey to find Keith was more than she or I could have ever imagined. We found each other as sisters as we searched for him.

Timeline of Journey to New Jersey
July 27 - August 3, 2013

Friday
Flew into Newark, New Jersey
Settled into hotel in Summit, New Jersey

Saturday
East Orange Library
Senior Center
Tent Revival

Sunday
Attended Mount Fountain Baptist Church

Monday
Newark Hall of Records
Planned to visit Montclair Historical Society but they were closed

Tuesday
Montclair Historical Society

Wednesday
Visited Newark School of Dentistry

Thursday
East Orange Campus High School

Friday
The Children's Home Society of New Jersey

Saturday
Rested, Relaxed, Reflected on God's goodness and mercy

Sunday
Returned to Atlanta

MAP OF NEW JERSEY

Cities that were part of the journey include the following: Summit, East Orange, Newark, Montclair, and Trenton. Keith was raised in Plainfield, a short distance away from where we searched.

CHAPTER 8
Clues at The Library

We arrived in New Jersey on a Friday and the search for Keith rolled out that Saturday morning. Elaine and I prayed, dressed, and started out for East Orange to locate the library. MapQuest in hand, tokens for the toll booths and a delicious breakfast under our belts, we began the routine we would use every day of the search: Pray, read the map, check that we had gas and tokens for tolls and then begin. Our destinations for the entire week were no more than a 15 – 30 minute drive, but seemed like forever as we traveled around to the different locations. Our goal for the day was to visit the library, a senior citizen's home and find a church to attend the next day.

Our first stop was the East Orange Public Library. Why the library? I decided most libraries might have accounts and records that gave information about any black dentist who may have practiced in the 1950s. Over and over I repeated to myself and to others "There weren't that many black dentists!" The dentist in my head was the assumed father of the "face" that I'd found in the East Orange High School yearbook. This was what I considered to be my first clue. The young man graduated from East Orange High School and the assumed father was a dentist I needed to find in the East Orange phone book.

Just as we came off the highway exit, we noticed a tent revival happening and I thought, "I know someone in that crowd could have known an African American dentist who lived and worked in the city." The crowd was mixed age and race. People were sort of milling around waiting for things to happen. The thought hadn't even occurred to me that Keith's family could have lived someplace else after moving away from East Orange, and no one at this tent revival may have known them.

Since I planned to go to the library first, I was really hesitant to stop, but I did just to find out how long the event or crowd would be there. I asked a few people and they said they were planning to be there all day. The event seemed fairly loose and fluid so I felt my sister and I could, at some point, join the festivities and discreetly ask questions. Hopefully we could get some ideas, names, and leads.

We left the tent meeting and traveled on to the library, which was just around the corner. We met a very helpful reference librarian and she offered us a private room to do our research. This was our first unannounced visit of many. We made only one appointment the entire trip. The reference librarian was the first person I shared the search with and from that point on, neither she, nor anyone else, refused to help, or thought it was a hopeless attempt with so little information.

God blessed us with people on the journey He wanted us to meet and relate to. Every person said something like, "Wow this gives me goose bumps." Someone said, "With computers now it makes it a lot easier to find people!" Of course, they were correct. However, it was the people I met who were using computers that encouraged me the most. At the library I found the same yearbook that I had found online with the young man's picture and one other picture I thought could have been Keith. I must admit that I focused on this picture as surely being the baby I gave up for adoption 57 years ago. He looked like he could have been my son with his father's features, too.

We left the library with a lead on a young man who'd just done a workshop on historic East Orange. I left my number with the librarian and looked forward to talking to him. I was given a few names and this encouraged me, but the last names were not Campbell. Campbell is the last name of the young man whose photo I found searching in the yearbook. From the very beginning of the search, I felt I'd find the key to locating Keith. I considered every encounter special.

Heading to the car, we saw a senior high rise building. Folks were sitting out in the sunshine in wheelchairs. We parked and walked up to the seniors, said hello and told them who we were looking for. One of the nurses shared that she had never heard of the dentist I was looking for, but she was under 30. I asked if I could go inside and talk to some of the seniors I could see in what looked like a recreation room. They were playing cards and looking at TV. We spoke with several of them about knowing a black dentist during the 50s. We also noticed that most of them had very little memory and no teeth. We left feeling a little disappointed and made our way to the tent revival.

We found the tent event livened with music since we left and people were eating. The microphone was being tested to start the program. There was a long line of people milling around waiting to be served so we joined the line. We talked to a well-dressed man who said he was a long time resident of East Orange but did not know any black dentists from the 50s. He did know that there was a large dental school not too far from where we were located and he gave me directions to Rutgers Dental School. Surely, I thought, they'd have records of former dentists in the state and whether they graduated from there.

My sister and I decided to stay at the event and ask more questions. We were also interested in finding a church to attend on Sunday. We found a seat and began to introduce ourselves to the people around us. We hit it off with a woman in front of us who was a local gospel singer. She was on the program and I thought that she would be a rich source of information. She was familiar with some local churches and as I shared with her, she recommended that we visit Fountain Baptist Church in Summit.

It turns out the church was right around the corner from where we were staying in the Grand Summit Hotel. She talked about locals attending that church with a large senior population and that some of them might remember the dentist I was looking for. I knew that my clues were short of information, but I trusted that someone would remember. I was sure to include the fact that the dentist I was looking for and his wife had adopted two bi-racial children. We left feeling we'd had a productive day. I had a lead on a young man who had done a workshop on historic East Orange, the name of a dental society, and a church to attend on Sunday. I felt that our first day of the search had been successful.

The next day, Elaine and I dressed for church, excited about finding one so close to our hotel, less than three miles away. We arrived and were greeted with friendly smiles and shown to our seats. The service was a typical African American church service. Lots of songs, amens, and "Praise the Lord." Early in the service, visitors were asked to stand. At that point the congregation began to sing a welcome song to us and my sister really got into it. She spread her arms and welcomed those in the front, sides and back of us. My sister is very animated and several people were smiling and egging her on. I said, "What are you doing?" She replied with a big smile, "I am welcoming them back!" She had a wonderful time that day, and no better place to enjoy yourself and the Lord Jesus Christ than at church.

CHAPTER 9
A Surge of Hope

On Monday morning, my sister and I gassed up the car, downloaded a Goggle map, made sure we had plenty of coins for the New Jersey toll roads and headed for Newark. Our goal was to visit the Newark Hall of Records and search for the African American dentist I believed was the adoptive father of Keith. My hope was that we would find him. I did think that the father might not be alive at this point but at least we would have looked and maybe, just maybe, we would find him.

We were fortunate enough to find parking near the building. I put more than enough money in the meter and we walked into a large old building. I did not know for sure what searching for this dentist would reveal. I had to start somewhere. I'd found a yearbook graduation picture of the young man who I decided Keith might have looked like graduating from high school. I know this sounds ridiculous and a little insane. I was trusting God and following leads that I felt came from Him. Often you believe that God has impressed you with something that you cannot ignore.

Finding the name of the dentist on the microfiche sheets, I hoped my visit at the Hall of Records would match the name of the man I believed was my son's adopted father to his. By the way, the dentist had the same last name, Campbell, as the young man's name I found in the high school year book. We were led into a room with large and dusty books and given a huge book with dentist's names, so we began to look. We did not find him in the books we were looking in and asked for some help. A staff person searched and couldn't find anything either. She questioned me again about why I was looking for this particular dentist and when I told her she said you might want to go down the hall, and ask to see the Director of Adoptions for the State of New Jersey.

My heart skipped a few beats. I had not even thought that such a person might exist and for him to be located right where we were was too much. My sister and I looked at each other and started walking the halls looking for the director. When we arrived at his door, we found him in the middle of a phone conversation. Over his head hung a scripture printed large enough to see that said, "I can do all things through Christ which strengthened me - Philippians 4:13,

(KJV)." I turned to my sister, thinking I was whispering, and said, "He's a Christian!" Mr. Peterson put his hands over the phone and said, "Yes, I am, come on in." We did not have an appointment and were just showing up to his office. Only a great God can orchestrate such perfect timing.

As we sat down and I began to tell him why we were there, he listened attentively and said, "I can't tell you anything because it was probably a closed adoption. What I will say is this, "Go back to where it all began." That was the first time I'd heard that remark and it would prove to be a pivotal statement of encouragement as we continued the search. We talked a little more about us coming to visit his church on Wednesday evening after I asked if there were churches that held Wednesday services. He gave us the church's address and directions and also stated that he would have his church pray for us.

I know the power of prayer and was touched that his conversation with us showed his trust and belief in the God who is omniscient, omnipotent and omnipresent. I felt confident as we left his office that I had been encouraged to continue to search and that somehow I was on the right path. I thanked him and we left. As we approached our parked car, I was shocked to see a police car parked alongside my car and a tow truck lifting the car just in front of mine. As I ran over to the policeman, I could see my sister out of the side of my eyes going over to the parking meter. She was pointing at it mouthing the words; "There is still money in there!" At the same time, I said, "Officer?" and he gruffly replied, "Get in your car!" I did just that as I looked at my sister, still waving her arms and pointing to the meter saying, "There's still money in the..." I interrupted her and through my teeth said, "Get in the car!" I turned to her and said, "Just pray!" She was still trying to tell me we had time in the meter.

Gathering my wits about me, I looked and noticed I had a ticket. I was afraid to get out of the car to get it, but I did. We drove away and I was shaking. I had to find a place to park and pray and thank God that I didn't walk out of the building at that time and find my rental car gone. All of the paper work and information about the car was in the car. I did not know what kind of car it was and had no idea of what it would have taken to find it. I've never had a car towed. I shudder when I think of what could have happened if my car had been towed. Praise God for His protection.

Later I asked others why we could have been towed. There was no sign that said we'd violated a city rule. I was told Mondays are street sweeping days in that area and cars parked there after 12 pm are towed. God was gracious and merciful to His daughters and rescued us. This could have turned into a disastrous day. This could have been a horrible second day on the journey to finding Keith. But God is faithful and He protected us.

Now I was more encouraged that I was doing what God wanted me to do: find Keith. We drove to a McDonald's and had another experience. I felt we needed to break for lunch and catch our breath. We went in McDonald's and tried to order. A Hispanic young lady looked at us wide–eyed and unsure of herself. As I ordered I noticed she appeared to be trying to read my lips, possibly because she couldn't understand English. I wasn't comfortable that she'd recorded my order correctly, but moved over for Elaine to order. The same scenario happened with her.

When our orders arrived, they were not correct. I tried to explain to her that the orders were wrong and she seemed befuddled. After a few minutes I asked another clerk if I could speak with the manager. I did not want to get the young lady in any trouble, but I did want our orders to be what we wanted. The manager quickly rectified the situation and apologized. When we found our booth, a young man came up to me and said, "I've never seen someone so calm and pleasant in here. Usually, when a clerk acts like that, people go off on them. You must know Jesus Christ." I told him that I did and it was no problem to be kind to her. We talked over lunch about the mighty acts of Jesus and how we are called as God's children to follow the example of His son.

I felt affirmed as a daughter of the most high God when I left McDonald's. The entire day seemed like a blessed miracle. We praised God as we drove away and thanked Him for His protection and care that day.

CHAPTER 10
More Searching in New Jersey

The third day of our search for Keith included beautiful weather and we were grateful. I loved the Grand Summit Hotel where we were staying. The hotel was a former Jewish Community Center and a perfect location for us. Elaine and I felt safe and could focus our attention on what we were there to do. We did not have to worry about looking like "tourists" who were easy marks. Every morning I offered up our day to the Lord Jesus and thanked Him for safety and wisdom. On this day we really needed God's protection, power, and provision. We would learn later why this prayer was very appropriate for this day.

Finding our way around with maps, coins for toll roads and an unfamiliar car was another story. We were often beeped and honked at around the toll booths. I was driving too slow looking for addresses and we were often confused about right and left turns. So beyond looking for my son like a needle in a haystack, we were trying to navigate East Coast traffic. My sister and I had a laugh later when she told me that she was not equipped to ride shot gun in New Jersey or any other place and couldn't believe I had the audacity to assign her that task.

Elaine and I started our journey to the Montclair New Jersey Historical Society, which is not far from Summit, but the toll roads were as difficult as ever. At our first toll I dropped the coins and had to lean over with the door open and retrieve the money. My phone slipped off my dress to under my seat and had to be retrieved. Meanwhile an impatient New Jersey driver began to honk his horn in the most obnoxious and disturbing manner. By this time, I was sweating and nervous. Once I deposited the money and the bar lifted, we were on our way at 50 miles an hour. I must give my sister credit. She was not upset or fussy. At no time did she say, even though she may have thought it, "This woman does not know what she's doing!"

As we rode along, I was not sure of our exit, so we exited, stopped at a store and Elaine got out of the car to ask for directions. We continued on but ended up still turned around when we saw a UPS truck. I immediately stopped to ask the UPS driver for directions, thinking he would know where we were trying to go, and another truck almost rear ended us. The truck driver shouted, "Lady you could have caused a very bad accident!" Later I realized that all of these circumstances could have been a deterrent to us getting to the Montclair New Jersey Historical Society.

I decided when planning the trip that a historical society might have information about African American dentists from the 50s. There could not have been that many dentists in East Orange. I initially tried to get in contact with the East Orange Historical Society. I found the name of the society's president with her picture on a website along with the mayor of East Orange at that time. The article was a feature story about the city celebrating their 100th year anniversary.

I got a phone number for the president and talked to her. Once I told her my story, she said I needed to put my request in writing to get more information about dentists in that area. I wrote her a letter, which included a picture of me and my family, and any details that I thought would help her understand my search. I also shared why I wanted to find Keith and how the historical society might help. I waited about a week and called her. She remarked, "Yes, I got your packet and I am so busy that I have not had a chance to read it yet. I'll call you when I get some time." I could tell I was dealing with a very busy lady. I was disappointed, and I never heard from her again. I began calling other historical societies in hopes that they might be able to help me. That's how we ended up going to the Montclair Historical Society instead of the one in East Orange.

Elaine and I got our bearings and headed to the Montclair Historical Society. There could be a record of black dentists in the area from that time. The ladies at the Montclair Historical Society were very helpful and excited. I was impressed with their interest and looked forward to meeting them. When we got there, we gathered around a large table with lots of photos of the African American community in and around East Orange and Montclair at that time. The society was located in what used to be the YMCA for African Americans in Montclair. The historical collection they presented us with was outstanding. We searched for clues for hours. Even the director and her staff joined in the search.

We really did not find anything of substance and it was getting late in the day and time for the office to close. Seemingly out of nowhere, a woman walked up to our table and said, "I am sorry to interrupt, but I've been listening to your story. I used to work for an adoption agency in the state of New York. What I can tell you is that you have to go back to where it started." POW?!?!?! This is the second time I've heard this same comment said in the same way by people who have and still do work in agencies that are involved with adopting children. She and the Director of Adoptions both said it with conviction, one day apart and in separate incidences.

I can truly say that a chill ran through me. I know God well enough to listen to Him when I sense He is speaking, especially when He says the same thing two days in a row. I thanked the ladies and told them I would let them know the results of my search. There was another little blip of possibility in our dentist search before we left the city. I learned East Orange did have one of the first African American Dental Societies as well as one of the first African American dentists who grew up in and practiced dentistry in East Orange. I located a female African American dentist by just calling around. I told her what I needed and asked if I could come to her office to visit. I calculated that Keith's father was probably in his 80s by now and had long since retired from practicing. If by chance he had been a prominent dentist, surely younger dentists would know him.

I smile now to think of how naive I was. Still, I pursued every hunch and clue that might lead me to Keith. When we arrived at the office, we were told to take a seat. Of course the dentist was busy. After about a half hour wait, an assistant came out and told us the doctor was so sorry, but she had given my request some thought and she did not have any knowledge about the dentist I was looking for living in East Orange.

We were disappointed and left there feeling just a little upset. Up until this day, most people had at least come out to talk to us. We felt rejected and as though we were not making any progress. We went out to eat lunch and prayed for more success at the Newark Dental School in East Orange. When we arrived we were able to speak to the registrar. It seemed she had records of graduates and dentists practicing in New Jersey from way back. She combed her files but could not find the name of the dentist we were looking for. Back to square one we went.

My original idea of finding black dentists to somehow find Keith's father didn't yield any fruit. I realized my search at the historical societies for him was not what I needed to focus on. I needed to go back to where it all began. Elaine and I talked about when to go to Trenton, where it all started for me and Keith. I made the decision we would go on Saturday. Previously I did all the research I could in Trenton and had no leads whatsoever. Going back seemed like an odd change of course. But back to Trenton we decided we'd go. While there I hoped to visit my father's last living sibling.

I did not know my sister had been on a search for our youngest sister Anna's son that she'd given up for adoption using Florence Crittenden Home, too. She had kept the information for 10 years and had decided to bring it along for our trip! She mentioned it to me and I read the letter, noting that the Children's Home Society agency had now somehow merged with Florence Crittenden. I was stunned. Could this be a place that I could go back to and get closer to finding my son? I called to see if they were open on Saturdays and they weren't. So I decided that we would go on Friday. I was excited about the possibilities of returning to Trenton "where it all began."

CHAPTER 11
Could This Be Keith?

As Elaine and I continued our search for him, I was sure Keith had graduated from East Orange High School and maybe I could find info about him there. The name was now East Orange Campus High School (EOCHS) and changed as several schools combined and moved onto the campus of a former college. Since it was summer, I feared the school might not be in session. I called and was told the school would be open until 1:00 pm and that the school secretary would be able to talk to me. My sister and I left early for EOCHS, which was less than a half hour drive. As always on this journey we had our map and tokens. We found the school without making too many wrong turns.

EOCHS is a large rambling campus that reminds me of my high school years, years that were fun and carefree until I discovered I was pregnant. I enjoyed many things about my high school and one of the best things was Sports Night. I danced and participated on the Red Team. All the girls could participate and join either the Black Team or the Red Team. I chose the Red Team. Competitions were set up between the two groups. Modern dancing, acrobatics, relays and a variety of sports activities demonstrated our skills and abilities. The teams were judged and at the end of the event the winning team was announced. I remember holding my breath along with my teammates to see if our team won. If we lost, tears of sadness would fill our eyes, but if we won, tears of joy would wash our faces. We stood still and listened for the results, then the whole stadium would explode into cheers or boos, depending on which team won. Those carefree and fun days are long gone but the memories are sweet.

We found parking at EOCHS and I noticed a very tall African American man directing a white man pulling boxes and loading them onto a dolly. We walked up to the two men and greeted them. I introduced myself as being from Atlanta and my sister, Elaine, from Detroit. The African American man said, "Hello." I told him that I had an appointment with the school secretary and asked how to find her. He showed me where to go through the door at the bottom of some steps. Why I felt it was important to ask this question, I'll never know, but somehow his height, confident bearing and authoritative voice led me to believe he was the principal. I asked him his name and with hesitation he told me. Then I asked if he was the principal. He responded with a cautious attitude, "You ask a lot of questions!"

Actually I was trying to be kind and thoughtful, not nosey. We had been so well received by the director of New Jersey Adoptions at Newark's Hall of Records and the staff at the Montclair Historical Society; I probably assumed I'd get the same reception. So I was a little taken aback. I smiled and walked towards the building. I did not want him to stop us from going into the school. I noticed my sister blinking her eyes and smiling at the principal. Through gritted teeth I whispered, "Do not do that!" Elaine dropped her head, chagrined. I felt as if Satan would have used anything to keep us from getting into that school.

With the picture in hand of the young man that I found from the yearbook, who I thought was Keith, we entered the school and were escorted to the secretary's office. We introduced ourselves and were invited to take a seat and told she would be with us in a few minutes. The secretary walked out, introduced herself, and said that she only had a little time to talk. I assured her that we would not take up too much time. I showed her the picture as we walked to her office and asked if he had gone to East Orange High School in the 70s. She said, "Oh, I graduated with him. He was very quiet!" I had a feeling that I cannot explain. Then she said, "We are going to have our 40th high school reunion next year." My head and heart went immediately to a wonderful reunion with my son. I was positive that he was this young man. I asked her if she knew where he lived. She said she would pull his records. She went to the back of her office and came back carrying a folder.

In this day and age of privacy issues and stolen identities, I can only say that I was shocked later that day when I thought of how wonderful God is to have not only opened the door for us to go into the school, but to also be able to see what may have been Keith's high school folder. Not only that, but the secretary was going to tell me if indeed this was the child that I'd given up for adoption 57 years ago. The next question I asked was, "Is his father a dentist?" She said, "I don't know." Then I felt, in the pit of my stomach, a small seed of doubt and fear as I asked her, "When was he born?" Looking at the folder, she said, "June something, 1956."

"Oh!" I exclaimed, "My son was born September, 1956." She

42

dropped the folder on her desk and went right back to her work. I was stunned and silent. I gathered my heart together, thanked her and said to my sister, who was looking at me with her eyes stretched wide in sorrow, "Let's go." I was very sad. No, this was not my son. I think it was one of the saddest moments of any other moment on my journey. However, my hope was still in my God who had sent me on this quest and Elaine and I still had one more place to go: The Children's Home Society. God knew where Keith was and all I had to do was continue to follow His lead to that place. God is faithful and will do amazing and wonderful things for His children if we trust Him and wait patiently for Him to reveal His plan.

CHAPTER 12
The Children's Home Society

The Florence Crittenden Home for Unwed Mothers had closed records at the Mercer County Courthouse that had been destroyed and I was not able to find any help at either place. The Children's Home Society (CHS) would be our next step. My sister and I made the little over an hour long drive to Trenton without incident. We had spent the entire week navigating the Jersey Turnpike, paying tolls and following the Google maps. Going to the CHS was opportune. Elaine had tried to research a little baby boy that our youngest sister, Anna, had given birth to and within days given up for adoption. Elaine contacted them and she had a letter dated 10 years earlier in response to her query; the letter gave her details about how to go about locating Anna's son. She'd never followed up on the letter, but she kept the information and brought it along for this trip. This information would be monumental in our search for Keith.

Only God could orchestrate such a providential incident. We arrived a little after 12 pm, locating the office in South Trenton a few blocks from where I grew up. The office was located in the old Roebling Building on Clinton Avenue. I used to walk past that building on my way to junior high school. Little did I know at that time that those same buildings might house information that would lead me to my son Keith.

When we walked in, the receptionist greeted us and I told her that I was trying to find a son that I'd given up for adoption 56 years ago. I apologized for not having an appointment and she said that was not a problem. Shortly thereafter, a woman came out and introduced herself and escorted us into a comfortable office. After some niceties and informal conversation, I told her how I'd given my son up for adoption and that I was now looking to find him. I shared that I remembered taking him to an office located on Monmouth Street in Trenton, right up the street from a public school.

I shared with her how my friend and I hid behind a tree to see who came out. Even now, I am still grateful for the picture I saw of his adoptive father carrying Keith and looking down on him in a loving way, with a mother smiling at them both and to my surprise, a little sister skipping along beside them. It was a picture perfect family in my eyes at the time and all that I wanted for Keith. I also shared that I couldn't remember if he'd been born on September 24, 25, or 26.

She asked me if I remembered the name of the social agency that was used. I told her no, I did not remember. At that point she excused herself and said she'd be right back. A few minutes later she returned, looked at me with a sweet smile and said, "We did have an agency on that street. I see your name, I see his name, and I see his parents' names." I would like to tell you that I cried for joy or said something that indicated that I had heard her. I was completely silent, speechless, and overwhelmed. I did not feel anything, then. She continued to talk about the process of having the agency search for Keith. I was listening in a daze with my mind going in and out of the conversation.

I heard that $400.00 would need to be paid and a notary would have to come in and verify my identity. She continued, "The agency has a 95% rate of finding people that they search for," and on and on she went. I sat on the edge of my seat frozen. Finally, I came out of my silenced state when my sister asked "Since we are here, let's see if she has Anna's information, too." I remember thinking, "I am still trying to process what I just heard. Keith can be found through this agency: she is going to start the process. I've found him!" They did research Anna son's adoption, but no information about our nephew surfaced.

But Keith was another story. Almost to the rhythm of my heartbeat I felt, "I've found him, I've found him, I've found him." How? By going back to Trenton where it all began. As I notarized the paper work and paid the $400.00, I was told that I would be contacted by a case worker in a few weeks. I thanked her and we got up to leave. As we left the building, my sister was walking behind me. She told me the lady was calling my name and trying to catch up with us. I stopped and she circled around me and said with wide eyes, "He was born on the 25th of September." That's when I lost it. My knees got weaker as I walked to my car and I put my head on the steering wheel. I blew out a sigh of relief. Keith's whereabouts would soon be revealed to me. **He was found. He was FOUND.**

After all these years and many hours of researching online, phone calls to agencies, time and energy expended, I was finally at a source that had his name, my name, and the name of his adopted parents. I was reminded of his correct birthday. The search was bearing fruit. I felt a real sense of awe in that God had divinely led me to the Children's Home Society. This was the place I'd been drawn to for the last week. Every encounter, every word of prayer, and every thought had led to this moment in time. Keith was not located, but able to be located by the information that had just been found. My sister and I left there elated, rejoicing and praising God for His faithfulness in providing and protecting us this far.

The Children's Home representative told me a little bit about the process. She was going to hand my case over to a caseworker who was, at that time, on vacation. She assured me that person would begin looking for Keith right away. I felt a sense of joy and assurance that this was going to be the beginning of an exciting adventure. I began to dream about the reunion, what Keith looked like, what kind of work or career God had given him. I thought about him being married with a wife and children. I longed to know that he was a child of God and worshiping the God I loved who had led me to him. I desired to know who his parents were and how they had raised him. Who was the little girl skipping along beside them and what was her life like now? At the time I did not know that she was adopted from the same agency and was just two years older than Keith. All of these thoughts were bombarding me as we drove away.

My sister and I were mostly silent. It was an unbelievable hour. We were so busy trying to find our way around Trenton that it was difficult to process what just happened. But I thought it was important to go visit with my father's last living sibling, Aunt Mercy. She was in her 90s and living in a nursing home. Her daughter Vivian came and led us to her room. It had been a few years since I'd seen her. Her health was failing, but her mind was still sharp and we laughed and loved on each other for a few minutes. Before we left my cousin Vivian, my sister and I prayed. We praised God and shared smiles of joy because of our visit together. As Elaine and I drove back to our hotel, our hearts were full and tears flowed so that it was difficult to drive. Our 10-day trip to New Jersey had come to a close. The process of finding Keith turned a beautiful corner and I was closer to my son than ever before.

CHAPTER 13
Returning Home

I began the process of waiting. I believe it was late August 2013 when my case worker called. She introduced herself and stated that she'd been assigned my case along with three others. She shared she was told, "Do this one first!" as her supervisor pointed to what was my file. I fell in love with my case worker immediately. She had a soft "New Jersey" accent that was so familiar, having grown up there; it was very different from the southern accent I've heard in Atlanta for 40 years. Her voice and attitude over the phone was a delight to my soul and brought back so many fond memories of my hometown and growing up.

Her first task was to interview me. We talked for almost an hour and a half. She asked me why I was searching for my son at this time. I told her that I'd always loved him and had never regretted my decision to give him up for adoption. Seeing him leave the agency with an intact family, including a little sister, was so comforting. However, I longed to know him and meet him and the timing was right for me to now do so. I also wanted to claim him as my child and reveal the long kept secret about him to those I knew. One of the questions she asked me was how would I feel if he had not lived a good life or was not living now? I remember saying I understood because those things happen in life. However, I truly did not think that there was any possibility that he was not alive and doing well.

She called me often with updates on her search. She was having trouble finding anything on Keith and said that was unusual. We know that with computers today you can find almost anything or anyone. However, she was having difficulty. I did not think too much of it. One day she called and said his adopted father had been located and was now deceased and she was not able to locate his adopted mother.

In mid-September 2013, I was on my way to Cedine Ministries in Spring City, Tennessee for a ladies' retreat. I've volunteered and served as a Ladies Retreat Committee member since 1998. My cell phone rang while I was driving and I couldn't answer. When I was able to stop, I saw there was a message from my case worker telling me to call her. When I called back, I left a message saying I was on my way to a ladies retreat and would return home on Sunday. I also said, "I hope you've got really great news!" After leaving that message, my cell phone rang; she was calling me. She asked me what I was doing and I told her that I was on my way to a ladies' retreat. She asked what it was about and I shared that Cedine Ministries was on a beautiful site in the Watt's Barr area of Tennessee where kids, ages 8-18, could go to camp in the summer and learn about God, Jesus his son, and the Bible. I continued with the fact that there were ladies' retreats, men's retreats, and couples' retreats as well.

As a member of the ladies' retreats committee, I help plan and support five ladies' retreats a year. Depending on the need, I volunteer to be the main speaker, emcee, workshop leader, small group facilitator, and sometimes just a help wherever it is needed. My case worker listened and said, "Tell you what, why don't you call me on Monday when you get back." I agreed to do so without a thought of anything being awry.

As I traveled home from the retreat that Sunday afternoon, I looked forward to resting on Monday. I had promised my case worker I would call her on Monday. I consider Mondays to be my day of rest and reflection for the coming week. So it was not unusual that I convinced myself not to call. For some reason I will never be able to explain, I just could not make the call. When Tuesday rolled around, I decided that the next day, Wednesday, September 25th was Keith's birthday so I wait to call, thinking a Wednesday call would be a celebration.

Around 10 am on Wednesday, two days after she wanted me to call her, I got a call from my case worker. She greeted me and I detected something in her voice that even now causes me to shiver. After our greeting, I told her I was sorry for not calling her. She seemed to quickly say, even blurt out, "Joyce, Keith is deceased!" I must say that I heard her, but I felt as if she needed to repeat it to make it real to me. "Did you say dead?" She responded, "I said he is dead." Silly question, I thought to myself, since deceased means dead. Somehow I did not want to hear her say it again. One time is enough to hear that the child you gave birth to 57 years ago and that you had earnestly hoped to find alive and well was dead. The child you wanted to meet as an adult along with his family was dead. The dreams I had of finding him alive died as well that morning. I had to continue to listen. Through my tears and hurt my case worker tried to answer some of my questions.

She continued, "He died in 1993 and has been dead for 20 years." By this time, I am in full blown crying mode and yelling, "No, no, no! What happened? How did it happen?" Words came out of my mouth but I honestly don't know if I made any sense. My case worker was kind, patient, and caring. She wanted to know if anyone was there with me and could I call someone? I assured her my daughter was near and I would call her when we hung up. I was hungry to hear the details. She knew he'd died of AIDS (Acquired Immune Deficiency Syndrome) but she had no further details. She stated that she was going to get in contact with his sister, the little girl I saw skipping along beside her parents and maybe she would have more information for me. What a sad day this was and definitely not what I expected.

CHAPTER 14
Talking to Keith's Sister

I heard from the social worker that my son had died, but she wasn't sure why and what the circumstances were or could have been. She told me that she would contact, Lynn, his sister, to see if she wanted to share more about Keith's life with me. It took about a week for her to contact Lynn, get her permission and for Lynn to contact me. I met Keith's sister over the phone. She sounded happy to meet me and started talking right away. It did not take her long to say, "He loved that lifestyle. He was gay and lived the lifestyle to the hilt." Imagine, if you will, my shock and, yes, my disappointment. She began to talk about him and I tried to process what I was hearing. One thing seemed to overshadow her voice, and it was hearing over and over again, "He was gay!"

Now I was hearing details about my son's life. His full name was Keith Charles Milligan. His father's name was Percy and his mother's name was Dorothy. I later learned I may have been told the family lived in upstate New Jersey. I found it interesting his parents kept his first name Keith because his mother liked that name. Many parents experience their child coming to them and telling them that being gay was their lifestyle of choice. I did not have that opportunity. After finding out that he was not alive, I still hoped to hear that he'd lived and enjoyed a prosperous, godly and fruitful life. As I listened to Lynn I could barely hear the rest of what she was saying. I wondered if my son's life would have been, could have been, should have been different if I'd kept him. Regret and doubts set in as I pondered...WHAT IF?

Lynn shared with me that he was a talented writer and loved fashion. I tried to locate some of his writing but have not been successful. He attended an exclusive co-ed private school in upstate New York from approximately 6th grade through 12th grade. Lynn stated that he attended Pratt Institute in New York, too. However, I've not been able to verify that information. I called the school but they did not have any record of him being enrolled. Keith traveled and lived in Paris, San Francisco and SOHO, New York. He worked as a window dresser at Macy's and other high-end stores. Lynn shared that Keith had lots of friends. At one point she stated that he wanted to move into his mother's house with his lover and that she allowed him to do so. She said Keith's lover died before he did.

I mentioned talking with Keith's best friend earlier in my story. She knew him from elementary school and initially she was hesitant to talk to me. She wanted to know why I was asking about Keith. I reassured her that I was not looking for salacious information, but felt God wanted me to know about him and his life as an adopted child. She eventually, and a little reluctantly, began to share. They went through elementary school together and were great friends. She stated that they were very close and did lots of things together. She talked about a trip they made to Atlantic City with a bunch of friends and how much fun they had. She shared that Keith was light-hearted and enjoyed singing songs from "The Wizard of Oz."

She told me that Keith's parents divorced when he was about six or seven years old. Before then they enjoyed vacations on Martha's Vineyard and from the picture I now have, had many happy moments around Christmas. Like most children on Christmas morning, Keith and Lynn were dressed up and seemed to enjoy their gifts. In one picture they had pet kittens. I sensed that they lived a very middle class life.

I know very little about Keith as a man. What I do know is sobering and many things are probably best left unknown to me. I believe God gave Keith a chance to know His love, pardon and forgiveness because of God's mercy and grace and patience. His friend shared that he wanted her to bring him some candy and a newspaper on the day he died. She did not get it to him in time. She said she did not attend the funeral either. She stayed at home; it seemed she did not want to see him in that state.

His best friend thanked me for giving Keith to his adoptive mother, and told me how much she loved him. It seems his mother spent time and money trying to find the very best care for Keith. She traveled to New York to get him when he was very sick and brought him home to care for him. It really saddens me to know how sick he became. He was always loved by me and deeply loved by his adoptive parents. I can only imagine how his adoptive mother felt as she watched Keith's body waste away. Earlier pictures of him show a beautiful little boy and a handsome young man. In the end, seeing his body, racked with pain and marked with the scars of HIV and AIDS, must have caused her much anguish and heartache. I understand from his best friend that Keith suffered greatly at the end, in addition to having lost many friends who also succumbed to death because of HIV and AIDS.

CHAPTER 15
Discoveries About Keith's Parents

Did I really hear the word "dentist" used to describe Keith's father at the adoption agency? Well, I believed that's what I heard. But I discovered later, from Keith's best friend, that Keith's father wasn't a dentist at all, but actually was a chemist. More than anyone, Keith's best friend from childhood revealed a lot about Keith's adoptive father and his mother. I was fortunate to be able to make contact with Keith's best friend when his sister Lynn gave me her phone number. I spoke with her and she gave me some insights into Keith's family life.

Keith's father was a parole officer and worked part-time as a chemist. So while I thought I heard "dentist," the word was actually "chemist." Keith's best friend shared he did not see a lot of his father but when he did, his father was very present in his life. He encouraged Keith to stand up for himself, like one time when he scolded him for crying when kids in the neighborhood picked on him. His father told him to go back outside and fight.

Keith's best friend remembers his parents divorcing when Keith was around six or seven years old. She shared she didn't see a lot of his father after that. Based on Keith's sister's account, she, Keith and their mother moved a couple of times in the city after the divorce. Instead of in East Orange, Keith grew up just around the corner in Plainfield, New Jersey. His best friend shared he did go to elementary school there and went to boarding school in upper New Jersey. He stayed at boarding school Mondays through Fridays for middle school and high school and came home on the weekends.

His best friend shared that Keith's mother was a parole officer as well as his father. She was involved in a lot of civic activities and enjoyed public speaking. They lived a middle class lifestyle and took family vacations in Martha's Vineyard. They celebrated Christmas and birthdays well. His parents were well known in the community as civic-minded and service-oriented people. If I had the opportunity to meet them I would have thanked them for choosing Keith. I would have let them know how comfortable I felt watching them walk out of the adoption agency with my three-month old son. I imagined they were happy with him and would take good care of him.

CHAPTER 16
Rewriting the Script About Keith

I imagined Keith growing up in a two-parent home with a family that loved him, provided for him, and protected his life. I pictured him living in a house with a white picket fence, and he did. I thought of him growing up enjoying family time around a Christmas tree and opening presents with a joyful shout because he got the presents he wanted.

I can see him going off to school for the first time holding his mother's hand and a little tearful that school might be scary. In my mind's eye he loved learning to read and playing on the playground with the other children. I hope he had good teachers who encouraged him to do his best. I was told he became a prolific writer. That pleases me because having to write makes me tremble. I love reading and I have a master's degree as a Reading Specialist. However, I don't like to write. Praise God for editors and people who helped me write on this journey.

I can imagine his parents being very proud of his academic achievements as I was of my other two children's accomplishments. I pictured Keith's parents giving him rewards and presents to encourage him when he disappointed himself or his parents with grades that were not good. I delighted in seeing my two children do well and achieve awards, win ball games, and accomplish their goals. I would have been just as proud of Keith.

One day I realized that I had to rewrite the script in my head regarding Keith. My heart trembles to think of how they felt when Keith revealed that he was gay. Did Dorothy recoil, cry, or reach out for him and tell him that she loved him no matter what or who he decided to be? I hope before this book is published I'll get a chance to talk to a mother who has been through what I believe Dorothy must have gone through. Of all the things I know about Keith and don't know, I'd like to know what happened that led him to become gay.

I saw the movie "Philomena" (Coogan, Pope & Frears, 2013) and it is so like my story. I've read the book "Philomena" written by Martin Sixsmith, which gives much more detail than the movie. It tells the story of an Irish woman who gave her son Michael up for adoption and her journey to find him more than 50 years later.

Michael was adopted by an American family along with a little girl he was very close with at the nunnery. They both lived there with their birth mothers. His adoptive parents had other children in the home when Michael and the little girl joined their family.

There is a part of the book that shares the subtle changes that came over Michael as he was growing up in America. He was a loving and trusting boy, quick to smile, and give a kiss to anyone who asked. But at some point early in his arrival in the states, he changed. Something very striking caught my eyes as I read Philomena's words:

"The first months in America, Mike was an enigma-one moment loving and affectionate, the next withdrawn and rebarbative." (I had to look this word up because I'd never heard of it.) It means: repellent, irritating, fearsome, forbidding, causing annoyance, disagreeable to the senses, mind or feelings, an unpleasant personality, prickly, spiteful."

Of course, in my mind I thought about Keith and his early years with his family. How was he emotionally affected? What were his feelings after being told he was adopted? Did he long to find his "real" parents? Did he wonder about his adoption, why and who "gave him away?" Did that make him search for love and connection wherever he could find it?

I thought about Lynn as they grew older. Did his moving in with them alter how her parents treated her? Now she had to share them with a little brother. How did their home change with a new baby in it? In Philomena's story, things did change for her son in his new adoptive family. Michael was five years old and his other siblings had to learn to share their home, bedrooms, and their parents. Privacy issues became evident and fights broke out.

All of this is normal in a family. They were trying to be nice to the newly adopted children, since there were two new siblings, a little girl, and Michael. When his parents met Michael, he had a little friend that would not be separated from him. They had to adopt her, too. She had difficulty speaking and cried constantly. The book shares that the youngest child in Michael's new family was angry and did act out because of the attention paid to the two new siblings. Later readers learn he did resent Michael at times.

I wonder how Lynn accepted Keith. Lynn was only two to three years older than Keith. When I saw this cute little girl skipping along beside her parents looking up at her new baby brother, I saw joy on her face. Even at a distance I could tell that she was happy. However, in one of the photos that I have she seems to not be so happy. She seems hurt, disappointed, and angry. Based on stories that she has told me, Lynn rebelled at an early age. I wonder if Keith was rebellious, too.

I learned that Lynn, as a young teen, found their adoption papers. She confided in me: "I was snooping around in my father's stuff." She confronted her parents and I am not sure how they answered her. She did not say what age they were when they learned they were adopted. I wonder if learning about your adoption at an earlier age is much easier than finding out once you become a teenager.

Once while listening to a radio talk show, I heard a young man sharing how he looked for his birth mother. He wanted to find her because of a medical issue. When she was located by the social agency, she told them that she did not have a son. I could hear his voice crack as I listened. She did like I'd done in college if I was asked "Do you have a child? I said, "No, I do not have a child!" That was at least a half true statement. Keith did not live with me. I had not raised him. So in my mind I did not have him.

My heart was weeping for that young man on the radio show. As he continued talking, he told the commentator why he wanted to meet his birth mother, hug her, and thank her for giving him to a lovely and wonderful family. He wanted her to know that he cared about her and in her old age he would love to be able to meet any need she had. I was so overwhelmed I drove with tears swelling up in my eyes. I began to pray and talk back to the radio at the same time.

In my heart and head I thanked the young man and told him I'd let him find me, if he were my son. I thanked him for loving his mom and wanting her to know him. I realized that since Keith was not living, I'd never hear him say these words. So I pretended that the young man was speaking to me. I said, "I'd love to meet you, and I love you and want you to know that even under the circumstances and results of your being given up for adoption, I love you, always have and always will. With all my heart I want this book to bless the hearts of birth mothers and their children to understand that no matter what the circumstances surrounding the birth parent giving up a child for adoption, it's all in God's plan for their lives.

I remember the girls I met in the home were from all kinds of backgrounds, races, colors, and creeds. I've thought about the college girls over the years and wondered what their lives turned out to be after giving up their babies. Did they think about their child often, for example, on birthdays, as they raised their own children? I wondered if in their later years some of them were not able to have children after giving birth to the first one and regretted giving up their only child. I imagine that some of them may have tried to find their child as I did. I hope their adoption search proved fruitful and their grown child, and with possible children of their own, was willing to accept their birth mother.

God used that day, listening to the young man on the radio, to assure me that He loved me beyond me ever hugging my son or hearing him say a word. God is so able to set up circumstances so that we know His heart is for us and that suffering has great rewards. I didn't have the chance of knowing my son or him knowing me. One thing I do know is God pursued me and changed my life through His son Jesus for His good and glory. I made the best choice I could when I chose to give Keith to a family that could provide and take care of him. I realize that I may not have been able to provide for him and care for him as his adopted mother Dorothy did in his sickness with AIDS. I realize that his choices were his to make, but as a Christian and also his birth mother, I am compelled to love him and others like him, and to look at them with compassion and with thoughtful prayers. I came to a point where I began to finally see Keith as he really was and not as I wanted him to be. He was his own person with a life that was his to live.

CHAPTER 17
Trying to Understand Keith's Life

I've had a difficult time seeing Keith as a young man being a part of the homosexual community. I struggled with whether or not he was molested and who introduced this lifestyle that eventually killed him? Some gay people share that when they were younger they were abused sexually, which confused their sexual identity. I will not know about the life he lived that was fun, creative and caring, about his family and friends. What were his likes and dislikes? What sports did he play and what teams did he cheer for? What were his favorite foods, colors and songs? In one very blurred picture of him as a young man he is standing with a bicycle and I would guess that he may have been a cyclist. That is just a guess, though.

I also wonder about him as a young man growing up in a middle class neighborhood. It appears he had many material things like a nice home, clothes and schooling. I was told he had many friends and was well liked by them. But was he teased for the way he acted, talked, walked? Was he openly gay or in the closet as a youngster? Whom did he confide in and who, if anyone, tried to encourage him to live a straight life? Did anyone talk to him about sexual integrity and how to live a chaste and/or celibate lifestyle? Were his parents trying to convince him to change his lifestyle or be who he wanted to be? Who else in his life had an influence on him? Was he ever on a spiritual journey? What foes and woes did he experience? And most of all, did the love, mercy, and kindness of God that is shown to all influence him?

Because I know very little about this time in his life, I can only conjecture what his life was like. Did he take time to ponder who he wanted to be? Did he seek help when he first realized the lifestyle he was living was not what God wanted for him, especially when he was sick and dying? Did he ponder how life may have been different if he had made different choices? Did he want a family or children? For many years I prayed for his family, wife, children, career choices. I prayed for his spiritual life, church family and how he was involved in spiritual things. I guess I did this because I wished it for him. I guess I wanted so badly for him to live a godly life, being successful and committed to God. I prayed for his salvation and for his family to be saved, too.

I prayed for him the same things that I prayed for his sister, Jana, and his brother, John. I wanted so much more for him. I just wished it for him. No matter what he turned out to be, I loved him and he's still my son. I had things in my mind, but those were the things that I wanted for him. He could have fulfilled the dreams as a husband and a father, but what if he was a philandering woman chaser or an absent father? The prayers I prayed still would not have been fulfilled. Our loving God, and he alone, knows the plans for our lives.

CHAPTER 18
A Letter to Keith

November 2015

Dear Keith,

Five years ago, your sister Jana, who is nine years younger than you asked me this question: "Mom, if Keith comes looking for you and you are not living, why don't you write him a letter?" Explain to him why you gave him up for adoption and what you hoped to give him through the gift of adoption." I pondered that request but did not write the letter then.

Several years later I began to pray, as I always prayed for you, about searching for you and what it would be like to find you. I prayed to be able to find a detective that would do the search. In February 2012, I found one who considered my request to look for you. Once we met and I told him the few things I knew, including that your parents were from East Orange and I believed your dad was a dentist, he said I did not have enough information and the cost would be prohibitive. My heart sank but I did not lose hope.

I prayed for you often, many, many times over the years, and felt a close connection to you. One day I specifically remember asking God to help me find you. I sensed the presence and power of the Holy Spirit saying to me, "I know where Keith is, and I can find him." I felt a sense of peace and contentment that indeed God did know where you were and how to find you.

Over the next year I began to think about how and where I could go to find you and I did go. This book highlights the places God led me to and the people who crossed my path during the search. The question that remains then is, why give you up for adoption and why wait so long to look for you? I can truly say that it was almost surreal. I read stories about children given up for adoption and then looked for later by a birth parent. I searched the web and found many stories about reunions that went well and some that did not go well where either the birth parent and or the child refused to recognize and acknowledge each other. I must say the latter did not deter me in the least.

After I gave birth to you in September 1956, I loved you

immediately, but had no real means of income or place to live. My great aunt Cora kept you in her daycare facility. She was, in a sense, your primary care taker. I worked for a department store and continued to dream about going to college. As time went on, I realized that I could not provide a home for you. I was living with my uncle and his wife, working and visiting you when I could. One day I came over to visit you and you were scooting along the floor with a full diaper dragging behind you. You turned your head and gave me the sweetest smile; I'll never forget it. In that moment my heart went out to you, Precious Son, and I said, "I need to do more for him. He needs a family."

I'd been told by the adoption agency that I needed to make a decision within three months. Time was running out, so I decided that I needed to let you go and hoped that you'd be placed in a home with loving parents. I did not know then that God was truly guarding and protecting both of us. In Jeremiah 29:11 (KJV), He says "I know the plans I have for you, plans for good and not for evil." Those words ring so true today, as they did then when I look back over my life.

I would have loved for you to know your sister, Jana and brother, John. Jana is nine years younger, and currently she lives in metro Atlanta with her husband and family. She is an attorney and practiced for 11 years in California. She currently home schools her two children Nathan and Paige. She is the kind of sister that would have been very caring and easy to talk to. I know this because she and her brother, John, are very close and can share and talk with each other.

John lives in Dallas, TX with his wife and two children. Cabby is in high school and Tre is in middle school. John is 12 years younger than you are. John is a pastor and teacher in special education. John played football and I believe the two of you would have gotten along very well. He is full of fun and loves to make people laugh. Both Jana and John are Christians and are raising their children in Christian homes.

I would have wanted the three of you to know each other. I would have loved to have the three of you together so I have devised a meeting of my own. When I put the three of you together in my heart, you have the same smile and Jana and you have the same look around your eyes. I wonder what you three would have been like as

.

young children, teenagers and adults. Would you have gotten along and shared life's ups and downs or would you have been estranged? We'll never know so I'll opt for closeness and friendship.

I remember saying to Jana and John once when they were very young and having a sibling rivalry moment, to not fight with each other. They were sister and brother and loved each other, so they could not fight. Many years later Jana reminded me of what I said because she took it to heart and they rarely fought with each other. I can see you in the mix now being the older brother taking charge and seeing to it that all of you got along. I can see you being the leader and comforter when they needed you. I believe you would have loved them and supported them in all their hopes and dreams. I believe you would have been the absolute best brother ever.

Loving you always,

Mom

CHAPTER 19
Blessing Others in My Journey

Trials make the promise sweet

Trials give new life to prayer

Trials bring to His feet

Lay me low' and keep me there

William Cowper, 1731-1800

Someone asked me if I had regrets about giving up Keith. Off and on, from time to time I have to admit I had regrets. I imagine that some of the girls from the home did indeed have regrets if they were never again able to conceive. I did not have my daughter until after five years of marriage. They may have tried to find their child as I did. But many women in other situations who have given children up for adoption have moved on, living their lives with family and friends who are not aware there is another child, a secret child, in that person's life. The pain of having disappointed parents, family and self by becoming pregnant and bearing a child out of wedlock can be very painful and shaming. I know this pain from experience.

There could be raw emotions of having been rejected by the father of the child who may have been someone you are now ashamed to mention. It could have even been a child of rape or incest. Your life changes forever and the looks and words of those who did not rally around you and support you may sting still. Maybe you were supported and loved throughout the whole ordeal. But you still remember that season as a painful and hurtful time in your life. I now know how much God loved me and how much He desires for me to take that suffering and let Him use it to glorify Himself and for me to use this journey to comfort others. 2 Corinthians 1:5 (KJV) reminds me of this: *"For as we share abundantly in Christ's sufferings, so through Christ we share abundantly in comfort too."*

CHAPTER 20
Celebrating Keith's Life

I felt led by the Lord to plan a gathering of friends and family who did not know about Keith. I wanted to tell them my story of having a child as a teenager and giving him up for adoption. I wanted to share how God led me to search for and find him. Nothing came to mind so again I went to the Lord and asked Him how to finally come from "hiding behind the tree" and keeping the secret about Keith. God loves us and asks us to give up our pains, plans, priorities, and pleasures to ask Him to work in and through us to accomplish His plans. I prayed, "Please Lord Jesus show me how to glorify you in a "reveal" and celebration of Keith."

I selected April 5, 2014 to be the day that I would openly and publicly talk about Keith, what my life was like during that time, how I gave him up for adoption and how God, in His sovereign wisdom and love located him for me after 57 years. The entire journey of searching for Keith had been a God assignment. Telling my story to the 19 women present that day was a scary and humbling experience. The ladies that were invited included women from my church, some women I had discipled and led in Bible study, and women that I ministered with. My daughter, Jana, and my god daughter, Rhonda, were present, too.

The woman that discipled me for four years and my grief counselor were present as well. I felt very close to these women and felt they would be understanding and caring about what I was about to share. I hoped that what I'd gone through to find my son would encourage them in their own life and circumstances to trust God in every area of their lives. I prepared refreshments and after everyone was comfortable and seated, my daughter opened our time in prayer. The secret I'd kept for many years was about to be finally opened to an audience of Christian women and friends that had known me for all the years I'd been in Georgia.

This was the first time I openly told my story; the story of how I'd given birth as a teenager to a son. I called this event the "reveal." Keith was a part of my life that I shared with very few people in the past. My ex-husband knew about him before we got married. I told my children when I thought they were old enough to understand that they had an older brother somewhere out in the world. I started the "reveal" by reading the first chapter of this book. There was not a dry eye in the house. When I finished reading, I told them about how God had impressed on my heart to look for him, places to search, and how to search.

By this time, I'd visited his sister in Florida and had secured some pictures of Keith, so I passed them around the room. I shared how my sister and I went about looking for him in New Jersey by the prompting of the Holy Spirit, and how I ended up at the Children's Home Society of New Jersey, to go back to where "it all began." My heart's desire for this gathering was to share how faithful God had been to me and how He'd provided, protected, and given me favor in the eyes of all the people I came in contact with while in New Jersey. If you are reading this book, then you know I did exactly what the Holy Spirit told me to do. When I finished sharing, one of the ladies sang a song and another said, "Hurry up and finish the book. I want an autographed copy!"

The women gathered around me to pray with and for me. I felt a burden lift from my heart. I'd been obedient, told the story, and been accepted. One sister in Christ reminded me I'd been forgiven by Jesus Christ for engaging in pre-marital sex and now there was no more condemnation from me or from other people regarding that. I realized I kept the secret about Keith for so long because of the shame and guilt of having sex and getting pregnant as a teenager.

I encouraged each woman with a note card and envelope marked with a number to write a note of encouragement to me over the next year. If the number was one that stood for January and if there was a two that was for the month of February. I received encouragement throughout that year. Their additional assignment was to help tell my story with anyone they wished to share it with. I am overjoyed with how God blessed me with their cards, prayers, and words of encouragement. Oh what freedom I felt. I could breathe again, a sigh of relief escaped from my heart.

CHAPTER 21
Searching: I Found Jesus - Poem

Joyce Washington Bray

I searched for Keith and found him

Jesus searched for me

Jesus found me and saved my soul in the month of October, 1981

Jesus was looking forward to saving my soul.

He was looking forward to making me whole and bringing me to the Father

There, I would be fully known and know

How I searched for Jesus

I searched in His Word

I expect to find him daily as I experience time alone with Him.

He is always ready and able to meet me.

He ever lives to pray for me, sustain me and abide in me

There, alone in my prayer closet.

I reflect on His goodness, grace and mercy.

He never disappoints.

I knew Keith three months

I grieve his life and death

I am encouraged by the awesome peace and comfort that

God has given of Himself to me in Christ Jesus

Oh God, I am comforted in knowing I will see Jesus

Thank you for the Precious Lord Jesus being found in me by your good favor,

May I remain faithful to search for you daily and find you in the journey?

 In the midst of disappointments, doubts, and death.

May I be found searching for You.

CHAPTER 22
Days of Learning

God has been teaching me so much in the days following the April 5th event. The day after was incredible with Him meeting me at "my pool of Bethesda." There I realized and internalized that "there was no condemnation in Christ Jesus and I could, "Get up and pick up my mat," which for me was my concerns about being judged if people knew I had had a baby out of wedlock. I'm reaching a point where I can get over the past, pick up my mat of sin and shame, abandonment and rejection, hopelessness and betrayal, and walk. I can be healed like the man at the pool of Bethesda in John 5. NO MORE DENIAL.

I asked God for forgiveness many times over the years. But instead of walking in freedom, I hid parts of my truth from others and I thought, from Him. I could not hide from God. He met me and healed me of my sin, all of it. The word sin simply means to "miss the mark." God's love and plan for our lives provides protection and guidance for us when we miss the mark.

Often we miss the mark through choices we make that are not God's best for us. We want independence and to be self-reliant. He desires we live in relationship with him and rely upon him. God loved me and convicted me of sin, all of my sins, not just the ones I wanted to confess to Him. He forgave and put my sins as far as the east is from the west and I was totally and fully forgiven. It was finished.

Psalm 25:18 (KJV) says, "Look upon mine affliction and my pain; and forgive all my sins." Because I am offering all my sorrows and my sins to God, I am forgiven. Praise the Lord I had to learn there are no too big or too small sins in God's sight. Just being sorry and sad about our sins is not enough. We must repent and turn away from them as well.

The power of sin lingers like a stained outfit. The sins I committed against God had to be confessed. I confessed it was wrong to have sex outside of marriage. Like the psalmist David, I asked God with hope and awe to forgive me of all of my sins. God can and desires to forgive everyone. None of the sins I committed were too big or bad to not be forgiven by Him. He is the great I AM and the great forgiver of sins. Every lie, stain, thought, action will be seen by Him and forgiven by Him, we just need to confess that we need Him.

Lord let me not pretend one more day. By saying that I have two children only is a half-truth. When Keith was adopted I said I had two children. When I learned he was deceased, I said the same thing. Now, I will say I have three children and one is deceased. Thank you God for opening the floodgates and sending down the cool and refreshing rain of your love, forgiveness, and joy.

"For ye shall know the truth, and the truth shall make you free."
- John 8:32 (KJV)

CHAPTER 23
At The Pool of Bethesda

"There is therefore now no condemnation to them which are in Christ Jesus, who walk not after the flesh, but after the Spirit. For the law of the Spirit of life in Christ Jesus hath made me free from the law of sin and death. For what the law could not do, in that it was weak through the flesh, God sending his own Son in the likeness of sinful flesh, and for sin, condemned sin in the flesh: That the righteousness of the law might be fulfilled in us, who walk not after the flesh, but after the Spirit."
- Romans 8:1-4 (KJV)

One of my close friends gave me a very important letter after the "reveal" for Keith. She reminded me to cling to the promise in Romans 8:1: "there is . . . no condemnation to them which are in Christ Jesus." I wish I'd read the note and understood the significance of it on Saturday, just after the day of celebration. But God has perfect timing. Later, I read and prayed over it during some time with the Lord Jesus and He was waiting for me at my "Pool of Bethesda."

I read John 5:1-15 (KJV) where Jesus asked the man at the pool of Bethesda, "Do you want to be healed?' The man made excuses and Jesus did not comment on them but Jesus said, "Get up! Pick up your mat and walk." Jesus did not wait for an answer nor did he accept the excuses, but He knew the man's heart wanted to be healed. Jesus asked me the same question, He said, "Joyce, do you want to be healed and free of condemnation? Get up! Pick up your cross and follow me!" He did not wait for me to answer either. Nor did I hesitate. I will be, am being, and shall be healed. I said, "Yes and Yes and Praise the Lord!"

God stepped on the head of condemnation in my life. Satan did try to raise his ugly head. Jesus has already stepped on Satan's head. The condemner has already been defeated; the fear factor is crushed along with self-preservation, shame, and self-condemnation. They have been healed by the pool of Bethesda. It is finished!
God wants us to "walk in the light as He is in the light" 1 John 1:7 (KJV). Whoever lives by the truth comes into the light, so that it may be seen plainly that what they have done has been done in the sight of God. I am living with no shame or condemnation. Fear

shall not shut me up, cause me to hide or back down, nor keep me from telling what our God did to help me find Keith and set me free from the sins that I committed against Him, and only Him, so many years ago.

I let rejection of myself and rejection from others about that part of my life taint, color and leave a cloud of secrecy around me. Finally, from my head to my heart I am free. I raised having a child out of wedlock above God's healing and love of me through Jesus Christ who has forgiven me completely. I am precious to God and He used me to minister to so many women despite my brokenness. Even while I ministered to others the truth that God forgives and heals to the utmost, I doubted that complete and soul cleansing healing for myself.

What freedom and deliverance has come to me and through me by our heavenly Daddy. Even knowing and understanding Keith's lifestyle did not stop our God from loving him and giving him loving parents, a home, education, and 37 years of life. Thirty-seven years is a lifetime and God was surely patient and waited for him to live a life of acceptance in the Savior as his own. He would have forgiven Keith. Look at what HE did for me! All have made mistakes. We fall short of the glory of God. We all need a Savior. His name is Jesus. God saved me and I do wish that I knew Keith surrendered to the Lord. Oh how I wish. Maybe he did before he entered eternity? I don't know. But God does and He's still on the throne over all.

The secret things belong to Him and Him alone. I understand God's heart for me. I have it for others and now I am free. I am free to love his sister, Lynn, and pray for her and her family to live a life that glorifies God. As a result of my search, the agency has given her a free search to find her birth parents. Oh how I pray that she will accept that offer.

I'm overcome by a God who cared so much about me and my son that He even allowed him to be born. God orchestrated him being placed in an intact family, to be educated and live with parents able to provide for him. Then when the time was right, the great Omniscient God of the universe allowed me and even encouraged me to find him with very few clues. Even without knowing how to search for Keith, God gave me a plan that worked.

I know there are women who have aborted babies, women who have given their children to family members to raise, women who have left their babies on doorsteps, women who have been raped and women who have sold their babies for drugs. I pray that those women who hear this story will take heart and know that God is more than able to search for and find their children, forgive them of their sins and to set them free from secrets and the condemnation regarding what happened to them and their child. If they look to Jesus who is waiting for them at the Pool of Bethesda, they can be healed. He wants them to get up and be set free. Jesus is ready to heal, comfort and save. I've always had a heart for young mothers and children. Now he's given me a definite heart for young men. A heart to pray for them and petition my heavenly Father to bring them into His marvelous saving light and life.

What a Mighty God We Serve

Traditional African Folk Song | Author Unknown

What a mighty God we serve
What a might God we serve
Angels bow before Him
Heaven and earth adore Him
What a mighty God we serve

CHAPTER 24

Keith's Voice - Poem

In memory of my son
Keith Charles Milligan
September 25, 1956 – May 11, 1993
Joyce Washington Bray

I never heard Keith talk

Nor did I hear him speak a word

The first time he said, "Mommy"

Was not to me

I felt him touch me when he was born

I felt his soft white skin

They put him in the nursery

 I saw very little of him

I did see his eyes.

Large, brown, beautiful

I saw him look at me and through me

Peering at a Mom he'd never know

A Mom who was not there to hear him cry when he had a tummy
ache or

A boo-boo

He did have a Mommy, an oh so sweet Mommy, who loved and

cared for him

Until the end

I touched his little fingers, his toes, and his little nose

I kissed his tiny lips and then, too soon I let him go

With a whisper in his little ear, "Keith I love you so…"

Be well my son

Live in peace with your new family

Take the breath of life God has given you for His glory

Hear Him speak to you. I love you little one.

Did Keith ever hear God speak?

Did he ever hear His voice?

I never heard Keith speak

I never heard his voice

I pray that Keith heard HIS VOICE.

In December 1956, Keith was adopted and named Keith Charles Milligan. His parents kept the name I gave him.

EPILOGUE
Thoughts and After Thoughts

These scriptures helped me learn about God's character as I searched for Keith:

And ye shall know the truth, and the truth shall make you free.
John 8:32 (KJV)

Now faith is the substance of things hoped for, the evidence of things not seen...
Hebrews 11:1-6 (KJV)

For I know the thoughts that I think toward you, saith the Lord, thoughts of peace, and not of evil, to give you an expected end...
Jeremiah 29:11-13 (KJV)

Faith is the substance of things hoped for. The private detective told me, "You don't have enough information." God said, "Nothing is too hard for me," from his word in Jeremiah 32:17 (KJV). God can do the extraordinary in ordinary ways through ordinary people. People spoke words of encouragement by simply saying, "Go back to where it began."

Esther 4:14 (KJV) reminds me, "And who knoweth whether thou art come to the kingdom for such a time as this?" Keith's life was in God's hands all along. The days of our lives are His to use, fix, form and bring to fruition. Keith's times were in God's hands, as Psalm 31:15 (KJV) illustrates: "My times are in thy hand."

Life is made up of time. Time belongs to God. His time means seconds, minutes, hours, days, weeks, months, years, eons, ages. After 57 years minus three days, after three years actively researching, and after 10 days in New Jersey hunting his whereabouts, God led me to my son.

A one-minute conversation on what would have been his 57th birthday told me that I had both found and lost Keith.

A one-minute conversation told me where he was located and that he died 20 years ago. I was not expecting that, but God can find us at anytime, anywhere, in any situation.

In ONE MOMENT I learned he was not living.

ONE SECOND I learned how he died.

God, not my will, but yours be done.

I'm waiting on God to reveal more of Keith's life to me.

Wait on the Lord and be of good courage, and he shall strengthen thine heart: wait I say, on the Lord. Psalm 27:14 (KJV)

Trust God to bring things to a good end: because "This is the Lord's doing and it is marvelous in our sight." Psalm 118:23 (KJV)

So many questions flood my mind:

Would I have been able, like his adoptive mother, to care for him like she did, and to demonstrate the same kind of love and devotion to him?

Would I have the life I now have if I'd kept him?

Only God knows the answer to those questions and the secret things of life belong to Him. I trust Him as my God, trusting Jesus as my Lord and Savior and the Holy Spirit who lives in me. I am praying this experience, as amazing as it is, will continue to encourage others to search for their children or their parents.

"And we know that all things work together for good to them that love God, to them who are the called according to his purpose. For whom he did foreknow, he also did predestinate to be conformed to the image of his Son, that he might be the firstborn among many brethren. Moreover whom he did predestinate, them he also called: and whom he called, them he also justified: and whom he justified, them he also glorified. What shall we then say to these things? If God be for us, who can be against us?

He that spared not his own Son, but delivered him up for us all, how shall he not with him also freely give us all things? Who shall lay anything to the charge of God's elect? It is God that justifieth. Who is he that condemneth? It is Christ that died, yea rather, that is risen again, who is even at the right hand of God, who also maketh intercession for us. Who shall separate us from the love of Christ? shall tribulation, or distress, or persecution, or famine, or nakedness, or peril, or sword?" Romans 8:28-35 (KJV)

PHOTOS

Keith celebrating his first birthday with sister Lynn.

Percy Milligan, Keith's adopted father.

Dorothy Milligan, Keith's adopted mother.

The Milligans holding Keith's sister Lynn.

Keith and Lynn celebrating Christmas.

Keith with Lynn, their mother Dorothy (right) and relatives.

Keith and Lynn in rocking chairs enjoying television.

Keith and Lynn holding kittens.

Keith and Lynn's modeling portraits.

Keith's high school senior picture.

Keith with Lynn and her children.

Joyce and her sister Elaine (left) enjoying sisterhood.

RESOURCES for BIRTH PARENTS and ADOPTED CHILDREN

My search for Keith began with very few clues. Actually, I had two clues as I stated in the book. They were that he lived in East Orange, New Jersey and his father was a dentist. Eventually, I discovered that the only accurate part of these two clues was that Keith lived in New Jersey.

As it turned out, he grew up and lived in Plainfield, New Jersey which is just around the corner from East Orange. I believe that God wanted to show Himself strong on my behalf and allowed me to find him to glorify Himself. As I prayed and sought God for wisdom, knowing in my heart that I could not afford an expensive search, I sensed God whispering, "I know where He is."

From that day onward I trusted God to show me and lead me to him and He did. How you should begin your own search and what resources you can use are listed below. They helped me tremendously. Take heed and remember that you will not always get a positive response along the way. Do not let that stop you, don't get discouraged, keep going!

PRAY and ask God to show you how to search for your adopted child or birth parent.

KEEP A JOURNAL: Whatever you do for each particular day keep a record of it. Note the people you talk to and what they say. You never know what will become a clue that leads you directly to your child.

THINK: If you have any clues at all, begin to think through them and about how you can use them. I spent a lot of time thinking about HOW TO SEARCH.

QUESTIONS TO ASK YOURSELF: If you are still in contact with the child's father and he knows about the adoption, see if he has any clues.

What could your child look like at his or her current age?

Where was your child conceived?

Where was your child born?

How old could his adoptive parents be now?

Can you search for a birth certificate, or record of your child's birth?

Can you call and write the facility where your child was born?

If you know the social agency that handled your adoption circumstances, write them and seek information. There is usually a fee, but it is not too expensive.

You might run into dead ends, but even eliminating leads can be helpful; the process of elimination is a good way to narrow the search.

Additional resources and tips:
Libraries house a great deal of information that can be helpful.

Hall of Records: I used the Newark Hall of Records. Google your state or city to see if there is a Hall of Records.

Historical Societies: Most cities and towns have historical societies.

Use Google to find information.

Do not use online search agencies. I used one and it was a scam. I lost about $400.

Churches can be helpful and a good way to find people who've stayed in a certain community for a good deal of time.

YMCAs can also be helpful to connect you with people in a community.

Senior Centers could introduce you to older people who may remember the family you are searching for.

Fraternities and Sororities are helpful if the people you are looking for were connected to these groups.

Finally, PRAY, PRAY, PRAY.

I am praying that whoever wants to find their child, or if you are a child that wants to find a parent, you'll be able to do so by God's grace. Be patient and know that God's will for you is to trust His love and tender care for you and your child and or parent. That love never changes.

You may contact me. Email me at: AuthorJoyceBray@gmail.com.

Blessings and Peace,

Joyce Washington Bray

REFLECTION QUESTIONS

Chapter 1: Hiding Behind a Tree

Jeremiah 29:11-13 (KJV)
For I know the thoughts that I think toward you, saith the Lord, thoughts of peace, and not of evil, to give you an expected end. Then shall ye call upon me, and ye shall go and pray unto me, and I will hearken unto you. And ye shall seek me, and find me, when ye shall search for me with all your heart.

What does God mean when He says I know the plans I have for you, plans for good and not for evil?

Have you ever pondered God's good plan for your life and if so, what have you learned?

What has recently happened in your life to prove God's plans are good for you?

Read Psalm 119:68 (KJV) and reflect on God's "good" character and plan for you.

Chapter 2: Meeting Marcio

Matthew 6:33 (KJV)
But seek ye first the kingdom of God and his righteousness and all these things shall be added unto you.

I grew up without the consistent and devoted attention of a mother and father. I felt very much alone and abandoned. At an early age I began to seek love and attention from the wrong places.

Many people grow up in similar circumstances. You may have grown up in such an environment.

Did you seek for love, attention, and affirmation outside of God's love, peace, and direction?

God has something to say to you in John 14:18 (KJV) and Deuteronomy 31:8 (KJV).

How does reading these scriptures help you begin to trust God's presence in your life from eternity past until this day?

Chapter 3: Keith's Birthday

John 16:21 (KJV)
A woman when she is in travail hath sorrow, because her hour is
come; but as soon as she is delivered of the child, she remembereth
no more the anguish, for joy that a man is born into the world.

Birthdays have always been very special to me. To have given birth
to Keith on the same day that I found out he was deceased was
fortuitous. Accidental, by chance, random, maybe.

How do you respond to grief, agony, and disappointment in life
when things do not turn out the way you had hoped they would?
Read Psalm 119:67, 71, 75; Psalm 34:19 (KJV).

How have things that seem as if they are "afflictions" proved to be all
about God who is for you as opposed to being against you?

Psalm 27:10 (KJV)
When my father and my mother forsake me, then the Lord will take me up.

By the time I had Keith, I was without a father and a mother. God was gracious enough to give me another Mom and Pop. They loved me unconditionally. I can never remember a time, after they took me in, when they did not provide, protect, and be proud of me in all of my endeavors. After sending me through college, they became grandparents to my children and loved and enjoyed them as their own.

Pray a prayer right now for the precious gift of your parents.

Read Psalm 68:6 (KJV) and pray for God to "set you in families." It does not have to be a biological family. It could be friends, neighbors or a church family.

Trust God to answer your prayer.

Chapter 5: A Stirring in My Heart

James 1:5-6 (KJV)
If any of you lack wisdom, let him ask of God, that giveth to all
liberally, and upbraideth not; and it shall be given him.

Asking God to help you do something may be a little scary and
humbling. Looking for Keith was like trying to find the proverbial
needle in a haystack. Once the stirring from God's Spirit to look for
him began I was unable to stop it. Truly after all these years this
must be from God.

So, how about you? What is God telling you to do and or not to do?

Will you trust and obey or decide that He is too busy to hear your
feeble cry and does not spur you on to do His will?

Read Proverbs 3:5-7 (KJV). Which words best describe you and
why?

"Trusting"…"acknowledging"…"wise in your own eyes?"

Chapter 6: I Decided to Search for Keith

Romans 12:2 (KJV)
And be not conformed to this world: but be ye transformed by the renewing of your mind, that ye may prove what is that good and acceptable, and perfect, will of God.

Is your life set apart for God's glory?

Do you remember the day God sent His precious son, Jesus Christ, to abide in you?

If Jesus does not abide in your life and you are willing to learn how you can invite Him, please take a few moments and consider four simple points below:

How to Have a Personal Relationship with God

One: God LOVES you and created you to know Him personally. *"God so loved the world, that He gave His only begotten Son, that whoever believes in Him should not perish, but have eternal life."* John 3:16

Two: People are sinful, meaning that unholy actions and thoughts directed by our self-will have separated us from a holy God, so we cannot know Him personally or experience His love. *"All have sinned and fall short of the glory of God."* Romans 3:23

Three: Jesus Christ is God's only provision for people's sin. He is God's Son and through His death on the Cross, the blood He shed washed away our past, present, and future sins so that we can know God personally and experience God's love for eternity. *"God demonstrates His own love toward us, in that while we were yet sinners, Christ died for us."* Romans 5:8

Four: We must individually receive Jesus Christ as Savior and Lord; then we can know God personally and experience His love. *"By grace you have been saved through faith; and that not of yourselves, it is the gift of God; not as a result of works that no one should boast."* Eph. 2:8-9

If you would like to begin a personal relationship with God today through his son Jesus Christ, you can pray and invite him into your life right now:

Jesus Christ, I need you. I confess that I have sinned against you and have been running my own life. Thank you for dying on the Cross for my sins. Please come into my life, forgive my sins, and set me free from the chains of sins and death. Begin directing my life. Make me the person you created me to be. Thank you for answering my prayer by coming into my life and giving me eternal life.

If you prayed this prayer, these things are true for you:
1. Jesus came into your life.
2. Jesus set you free from the power of sin and forgave you for all of your mistakes and shortcomings.
3. You became a Child of God.
4. You received eternal life.
5. You began the new satisfying life for which God created you.

Welcome to God's family! Today is your spiritual birthday, the day you received new and eternal life through Jesus Christ. We celebrate our physical birthdays every year. Why not celebrate such a special day as your spiritual birthday too? If you already are a believer but cannot think of the day you were born again, select an appropriate date, and celebrate it yearly as your spiritual birthday.

DATE SELECTED: _____

Now pray a prayer of praise to God for His marvelous salvation, new life and desires. Read and reflect on Hebrew 13:15 (KJV): "By Him therefore let us offer the sacrifice of praise to God continually, this is, the fruit of our lips giving thanks to His name."

Next Steps:

- Find a church home to join.
- Read your Bible daily, begin with the book of John.
- Pray daily.
- Spend uninterrupted, undistracted time with God. Start with at least thirty minutes per day.
- Find a mature, Christian friend to share with and be accountable to on your Christian journey.
- Trust God by faith to help you grow and mature. Phil 1:6

Chapter 7: Finding a Sister in the Journey

John 8:32 (KJV)
And ye shall know the truth and the truth shall make you free.

Read John 3:16 and then read 1 Peter 4:8, "And above all things have fervent charity among yourselves: for charity shall cover the multitude of sins."

Read slowly and take in the compassionate love that God has for you. Realize that you are not consumed or destroyed, under His watchful eye.

Focus on His compassion for you and care for your soul. God has great love for us. We are made in His image and His love is everlasting. My journey with God, along with my sister, was filled with care, compassion, and love. I am so thankful and grateful for His love for me and my sister and our love towards each other. He has adopted both of us into His family.

Write a prayer of thanksgiving to God for how much he cares for you and your family. Pray especially for renewed and reconciled relationships.

Chapter 8: Clues at the Library

James 4:13-14 (KJV)
Come now, you who say, "Today or tomorrow we will go into such and such a town and spend a year there and trade and make a profit" – yet you do not know what tomorrow will bring. What is your life? For you are a mist that appears for a little and then vanishes.

Unexpected circumstances can really upset us and cause us to doubt God. Satan is the deceiver casting doubt, destruction and deception towards us. Count him out and count on God.

Our first day searching for Keith did not turn out to be what I expected and then again it was exciting and encouraging to watch God work.

Read 1 John 4:4 (KJV), "Ye are of God, little children, and have overcome them; because greater is He that is in you, than he that is in the world."

Think of something that is causing you to doubt, be deterred, and distracted from what God would have you to do.

Commit to following Jesus as Paul commits in 1 Corinthians 10:31 (KJV), "Whether therefore you eat, or drink, or what so ever you do, do all to the glory of God...Be ye followers of me, even as I also am of Christ."

Chapter 9: A Surge of Hope

Romans 8:28 (KJV)
And we know that all things work together for good to them that
love God, to them who are the called according to His purpose.

Consider the "all things" that seemed to be working together for
good at Newark Hall of Records.

God was directing me there and at McDonalds afterwards. What is
going on in your life right now that may be an "all things working for
good?" situation. It may not seem like it, but you can sense God's
presence and peace.

Can you stop and praise God now for how He is working things out
for your good? Remember, "Now faith is the substance of things
hoped for, the evidence of things not seen," Hebrews 11:1 (KJV).

Can you "hope for it" no matter what?

1 Samuel 15:22 (KJV)
To obey is better than sacrifice.

On this day God said the same thing that He said before, "Go back to where it began!" Can you imagine the thoughts that went through my head? One of them was that God really wants me to return to my hometown. It seemed that there was something to be found there and I felt drawn as if an awesome and powerful magnet was pulling my soul.

What do you do when God tells you to do something more than one time?

Do you obey or shrug your shoulders and dismiss it?

Can you remember a time when you obeyed God's gift of reminding you over and over to do something?

Pray right now to hear the voice of Jesus and be quick to obey.

Chapter 11: Could This Be Keith?

Matthew 7:7-8 (KJV)
Ask and it shall be given you; seek, and you shall find knock and it shall be opened unto you. For everyone that asks receives and he that seeks finds and to him that knocks it shall be opened.

I thought about Keith's parents often. I prayed for their well-being and that they knew Jesus, loved Him, and served Him. I am sure that they did the best they could. I know Keith was loved, provided for and given much that the world considers to be the finest.

But what about his spiritual life? Did he ever seek to find Jesus and know Him as Lord and Master? What about you?

As you ponder your eternal existence, are you a child of the God of the universe?

The God who made you in His image created you to live a life that glorifies Him. You can do that now.

Read Romans 10:9 and by faith, believe and begin a personal relationship with God through His son Jesus Christ, "That if thou shalt confess with thy mouth the Lord Jesus and shalt believe in thine heart that God hath raised him from the dead, thou shall be saved."

Chapter 12: The Children's Home Society

Proverbs 13:12 (KJV)
Hope deferred makes the heart sick, but a longing fulfilled is a tree of life.

Our day at East Orange Campus High changed the course of our search. Our hope was dashed, deferred, and disappointing. Doubt could have claimed the day.

What about you? Are your emotions in turmoil?

Are your dreams dashed and there seems to be no hope of recovery? Be comforted by God's word which is so very comforting, especially in Psalms. Read these scriptures slowly and meditate on what God is saying to comfort you. Write out the scripture and put your name in where it fits.

Psalm 55:22 (KJV), "Cast your cares on the LORD and he will sustain you; He will never let the righteous fall."

Chapter 13: Returning Home

Read Psalm 34: 15, 17, 18, 19, 22 (KJV)

Have you ever lost something that is very dear to you? How did you feel about finding what was lost?

Think of the journey God has you on up to this point.

There are many points of reference, but in every detail God was at work.

Think of how His attributes are working in your life. Ponder these three attributes. Pray for them to become meaningful and vitally alive to you today.

God is Omnipresent in your life.
God is Omniscient in your life.
God is Omnipotent in your life.

Now read and pray 1 Chronicles 29:14 (KJV) "…for all things come of thee and of thine own have we given thee…"

Chapter 14: Talking to Keith's Sister

Deuteronomy 4:31 (KJV)
For the LORD thy God is a merciful God; he will not forsake thee, neither destroy thee, nor forget the covenant of thy fathers which he swore unto them.

Are you a "waiter?" Not the kind that works at a restaurant, but a waiter on God. It took some time to hear whether or not Keith was found. So I had to wait.

What are you waiting for? What dream, hope, promise of God are you wanting to come to fruition?

Read Psalm 119:165 (KJV) and pray for peace in the wait.

Read James 5:16 (KJV) and trust God to see you through the WAIT!

Write out a prayer using both scriptures here.

Chapter 15: Discoveries About Keith's Parents

John 8:32 (KJV)
And ye shall know the truth, and the truth shall make you free.

I truly had to depend and trust God when I listened to Keith's sister for the first time. The truth was difficult to hear. However, I know that Romans 8:28 is a truth that may not always be understood. "LORD," I prayed, "How can this be 'working for good?' I want Keith to be alive and well and living a life that pleases You."

A selfish prayer? Yes. A mother's heartfelt prayer? Yes.

When and or have you had to trust and believe in a difficult situation?

Have you heard or experienced some news and you were disappointed in yourself, others and especially God?

What are you going to do?

Read 1 John 5:4-5 (KJV). After reading this scripture pray for God to defeat the enemy who has blinded the minds, hearts, and eyes in the community and lifestyle that Keith gave his life to.

Read and pray through 2 Timothy 4:18 (KJV).

Chapter 16: Rewriting The Script About Keith

2 Corinthians 1:5-6 (KJV)
For as the sufferings of Christ abound in us, so our consolation also aboundeth by Christ. And whether we be afflicted, it is for your consolation and salvation which is effectual in the enduring of the same sufferings which we also suffer; or whether we be comforted, it is for your consolation and salvation.

It is best not to know some things.

Even though I see Keith's lifestyle all around me on television, in my community, the internet, magazines, etc., it is still a surreal and difficult view of life and certainly more so from God's perspective.

Have you ever wondered how far and how deep you would go refusing to turn to God? Read through Romans 1 very slowly and picture the results of turning your back on God.

Pray for God to deliver you and rewrite your life script.

Chapter 17: Trying to Understand Keith's Life

Philippians 4:13 (KJV)
I can do all things through Christ which strengthened me.

What does this scripture say to you about the ability of Jesus Christ to help you? To help you do something that is difficult? Pray now for Jesus to help you in some trial, temptation, and or affliction you may be experiencing.

What does "all things" mean in this scripture?

List the things that may be concerning you and causing fear and anxiety.

Circle one and begin to pray for God to help you do "all things in His strength."

Chapter 18: A Letter to Keith

It may be time for you to write a letter. Is there a situation, affliction, person or maybe yourself that you need to speak to and finally say what's been on your heart?

These circumstances may be recent or in the past. Whatever the time, can you now write about it? Write whatever comes to your heart and do not censor yourself.

I pray that a strong sense of relief and rest pours over your heart and soul. I pray that your strength will be made manifest through the spirit of the living Lord, Jesus Christ. Begin now by starting this sentence, "Dear_____"

Chapter 19: Blessing Others in My Journey

Job 14:12 (KJV)
So man lies down and does not rise.

Death is so final. It was hard for me to hear the social worker say, "He is deceased!" I still feel the blunt blow to my soul. I desired to find Keith alive and well. I'd hoped for my son to have a family, good health and prosperity. All the things that life has to offer that are godly and good, I wanted for Keith. Instead I collapsed into tears of sorrow and regret, and imaginations about his illness and how his life could have ended so sadly.

However, as I've thought about God's goodness, faithfulness, and love I know God's plans are for our good and not for evil. Read through Jeremiah 29:11-13 (KJV) and meditate on what God is saying to you. Take time to think on the good that has come out of the different circumstances in your life that looked bleak and insurmountable.

Can you see the good that has given you hope, courage, strength, and wisdom to press on?

I hope so, because I found that hope, peace and courage.

As Job proclaimed in Job 1:21 (KJV) "The LORD gave and the LORD hath taken away; blessed be the name of the LORD."

Can you pray with assurance and peace, "Blessed be the name of the LORD?"

Chapter 20: Celebrating Keith's Life

This was a difficult and emotional day for me. I'd never publicly explained to people that I'd had a child out of wedlock. I invited 20 women to come to what I was calling a reveal. Seventeen women came including my daughter, god daughter, longest Atlanta friend and my grief counselor.

Some of these were women who had been on this journey with me and some had not. I'd always feared the looks on faces as I'd shared with a few people in my life. Today would be a test of trusting God and not considering the looks on faces. I felt and saw genuine love and concern for me as I shared how I gave Keith up for adoption, searched for and found him. There was not a dry eye in the house.

What is it you'd like to share and feel afraid to do so? Can you picture Jesus looking into your eyes and saying, "It's alright, I love you, my face is towards you and full of love and forgiveness"? Trust me to hold my arms wide towards you and embrace you no matter what."

In Luke 15:11-32 (KJV) read the story of the Prodigal Son and the warm reception his father gave him after he left his family, wasted his inheritance, and decided to face the music and returned home.

Do you need to face up to anything? Is there a secret you've been hiding and wanting to reveal?

Maybe you should start by just telling Jesus. He's quick to listen and longs to forgive. Do it now. The rest, peace, and comfort will come. Read the following scripture and meditate on the words.

Isaiah 30:15 (KJV), "For thus saith the Lord God, the Holy One of Israel; In returning and rest shall ye be saved in quietness and in confidence He'll be your strength."

Chapter 21: Searching: I Found Jesus – Poem

Psalm 118: 23(KJV)
This is the LORD'S doing: it is marvelous in our eyes.

Think of something you have suffered through and seen God use to grow and stretch your faith.

Write a PRAISE PRAYER as the disciples did in Acts 5:41(KJV) when they realized that they had been counted worthy of suffering disgrace for Christ Jesus.

Why not write your prayer of praise right now to Him for counting you worthy and showing you how marvelous He is to you?

Chapter 22: Days of Learning

Romans 11:22 (KJV)
Consider therefore the kindness and sternness of God: sternness to those who fell, but kindness to you, providing that you continue in His kindness. Otherwise, you also will be cut off.

God reminds me of His many attributes and His kindness is overwhelming. I experienced a multiplicity of kind acts while searching for Keith. Kindnesses extended by people who did not know me nor I them.

The most insignificant comment or kind deed may bring the best and most profound outcome. Simply hearing "go back to where it all began" twice in two days by two separate individuals was very inspiring. I felt the Lord Jesus pointing me in the right direction by both people.

Have you ever sensed God giving you directions and hope by His word, circumstances, or people?

How did you handle it? Did you obey and follow the prompting of the Holy Spirit or did you let the opportune time pass?

Remember the situation and your response. Let it encourage your heart to know that your prayers are often answered in surprising and wonderful ways.

Psalm 34:19 (KJV), "I will bless the LORD at all times; His praise shall continually be in my mouth."

Chapter 23: At The Pool of Bethesda

John 5:1-15 (KJV)

Have you ever sat down to have devotion time with the Lord Jesus and felt that He was right there beside you? As you read His words do you feel as if He is speaking directly to you?

What joy and peace came over me one morning, I sensed Jesus saying to me, "You are free." Take a moment and read through John 5:1-15. Read slowly and thoughtfully.

Do you sense God's presence, peace, and power? Let Jesus speak to you and let Him stretch out His hand and call you to grasp hold as he says, "Do you want to be made well?"

Oh, I pray that your answer will be, "Yes, yes and yes!"

Now, thank Him right now for setting you free on Calvary and know that "whom the Lord sets free is free indeed," John 8:36 (KJV).

REFLECTION QUESTIONS

EPILOGUE

I grew up thinking I was all alone. Mom gone, Dad gone. Who was there for me? As I looked back over my life the path I took and how things "coulda shoulda" been I know that God's hands were on my life all along.

He was always watching over me and never abandoned me.

I've found Him and I pray daily to not leave Him. I pray I'll hear His voice daily and at the end of my life hear Him say, "Well done good and faithful servant."

Will you write a prayer now to daily hear His voice and sense His presence in you, around you, and over you, to His glory?

What are you SEARCHING for?

Matthew 6:33 (KJV), "Seek ye first the kingdom and God and His righteousness and all these things will be added unto you."

ABOUT THE AUTHOR

I realized writing this book that I have been searching for family all of my life. My precious little granddaughter brought me to that realization one day as we traveled home from a Wednesday morning bible study when she was 3 years old. Every Wednesday I would pick her up. Some mornings she was eager to go and other times she'd complain the whole way there.

Usually we'd stop afterwards for lunch and enjoy a time of play for her in the children's play area of our local Chick-Fil-A. Afterwards, driving down her tree lined street we'd play a little game called, "Where do you live?"

I'd start with asking her, as I pointed to a house, "Is that your house?"

She'd reply with a smirk, "No Mimi, I don't live there!"

"How about this one?" I'd question her, knowing that she didn't live there either.

"No!" She'd shake her head smiling with the look of truly knowing where she lived.

So on and on we'd go playing our little game until we came to her house. As I pulled into the drive way she'd grin and I'd say to her, "Is this it?" "Yes!" she said with an emphatic nod of her head.

"Oh my," I'd sadly say, "No one lives here. Are you sure this is where you live?"

My granddaughter would stick out her chest and say with passion and assurance, "Mimi, I have a family, I live here!" The tone of her voice, smile on her face and assured response helped me to understand and appreciate that my granddaughter really knew what "family" meant. I felt so blessed to see how God had worked in her life and mine for good and restored what "the locust had tried to eat!" Praise God.

Early in life I grew up without a mother and a father. When I became pregnant at 18 I was lonely and needed the loving protection and care of a family. Over the course of that season in my life, as I reflect on God's goodness and plans for my life, I can see that He'd gone ahead of me and provided family. Different people played different roles as my needs arose.

Family that sent me to college, marriage with children became my own family and finally I became an adopted daughter into the family of God. Yeah, God! I've joined the heavenly family with sisters and brothers in Christ. I even enjoy surrogate grandchildren whom I love as if they were "blood kin!" When I count how many surrogate grandchildren I have, it goes way past my four and on up to twelve and counting. But it does not stop there. I have surrogate daughters galore and sons they are married to as well.

I have church family, ministry family and neighbor family and friends as family. I am richly blessed...I am more than richly blessed. Most of all I have Jesus, my Savior, Redeemer and Friend. So I praise God as the Head of my family. I have a passion for ministering to women who are carrying around guilt and shame. Women who need the love and compassion of a loving family.

I look forward to sharing with them how God can and will deliver. He delivered me as I once sat by the Pool of Bethesda broken, wounded, and sad. By His healing spirit I walked away free from guilt and shame. I am trusting that you, too, will be adopted into the one and only everlasting FAMILY OF GOD.

Today Joyce Washington Bray is an author, speaker and missionary. She resides in metro Atlanta. Contact her at AuthorJoyceBray@gmail.com.

Made in the USA
Columbia, SC
29 April 2017